Dreams and the Person-Centered Approach is a
on working with dreams that collects, d
main approaches found in the person-cen
addition to presenting these, Andrea Koch describes her own understanding
of "cherishing client experiencing" in dreams: a process of self-healing
by sensing into dreams and facilitating the meaning-creating process of
the client. Examples of dreams and their exploration from both the client's
experience and the therapist's perspective help the reader to find their
own way of "being with" the dreamer.

The book is a highly recommended, easily readable resource for
practitioners and students to help them to understand the world of their
own and their clients' dreams as parts of their personality development.
Peter F. Schmid, Sigmund Freud University, Vienna

This book is a gem! Andrea Koch has done a great service to everyone
interested in dreaming by showing how the person-centered approach of
Carl Rogers can illuminate powerful and transformative meanings in our
dreams. Koch's deeply empathetic method offers a wonderful resource to
therapists and counselors who may never have received any training in
dream interpretation but are eager to tap into the healing energies of their
clients' dream experiences. Well-researched and clearly written with
numerous examples and helpful advice, Koch's book is like a personal
seminar on working with dreams.
**Kelly Bulkeley, Visiting Scholar, Graduate Theological Union,
Berkeley, California**

Beware this book could seriously enrich your dream life! Shining light into
a previously neglected territory this book informs, stimulates and enlivens
edge-of-awareness processes both day and night. It brings a refreshingly
different approach to exploring dreams in a lively and accessible style. It is
practical, theoretical and imaginative and I can't wait to recommend it to
peers and counsellors in training. There's nothing quite like it out there.
Suzanne Keys, counsellor, group facilitator and trainer, London

Dreams and the Person-Centered Approach

Cherishing client experiencing

Andrea Koch

PCCS Books
Monmouth

First published 2012

PCCS Books Ltd
Wyastone Business Park
Wyastone Leys
Monmouth
NP25 3SR
UK
Tel +44 (0)1600 891 509
www.pccs-books.co.uk

Dreams and the Person-Centered Approach: Cherishing client experiencing

A CIP catalogue record for this book is available from the British Library

ISBN 978 1 906254 47 6

Cover artwork is 'Return' by Victoria Rabinowe, DreamingArts Studio, Santa Fe, USA
Cover designed in the UK by Old Dog Graphics
Typeset in Garamond in the UK by The Old Dog's Missus
Printed in the UK by ImprintDigital, Exeter

Contents

Dedicated to the next generation of dreamers,
among them Wanda, Mikaela, and Marilu

Acknowledgments

True to my first calling and profession – human geography – I want to start with acknowledging a very special place on this earth: the little island of Hiddensee. This gem, which lies in the Baltic Sea, has been a continuing spring for the most inspirational and creative thoughts in this book (as well as the dreams accompanying the process!).

Without Helga Lemke's phone call after she had just finished reading my master's thesis on dreams and person-centered counseling, I never would have considered being the author of a book. She suggested I submit the thesis to the German "Gesellschaft für wissenschaftliche Gesprächspsychotherapie" (the GwG is the German person-centered umbrella organization) and ask them to publish it. But the GwG wasn't convinced so I had the idea of writing a book in English; much more on the subject matter had been written in German, and very little in English. Also, it led me straight to a very supportive and enthusiastic publisher, Pete Sanders and PCCS books.

When I asked them if they would join me in this book project, all three of my "special guests" – Helga Lemke, Barbara McGavin and Clara Hill – agreed immediately. This was the next step into the "real world" after finding a publisher, and the sincere, positive and clear feedback of all three gave me an immense early boost.

After my dream session with Clara Hill, one of my action steps was to go out in search of help … I found many very capable and supportive editors of the book as a work in progress:

Abbe Blum, Katarina Halm, Barbara Kettnaker, Lore Korbei, Janet Pfunder, Elke Schönrock, and Alice Wang. Without their stimulating and helpful comments and feedback this book would have been so much less and I might have given up along the way.

I found many teachers and competent supporters in my person-centered, Focusing and dreamsensing journey. I would like to thank and mention especially: Dagmar Gösche, Lore Korbei, Angelika Kopečný, Dave Mearns, Janet Pfunder, Astrid Schillings and Ann Weiser Cornell.

My family, especially my parents, have been with me along the whole way. Although – due to the ailing health of my father – my mother has not been the first editor, as she was with my master's thesis and the *Person-Centered and Experiential Psychotherapies* (*PCEP*) article on dreams, she and my father have coached me through the whole process. I seem to follow in at least some of my father's footsteps. He wrote his MD thesis in 1959 on children's dreams – I am very sorry to say that seemed to be the end of his "love affair" with dreams; he never talked to us children about dreams until I started talking to him about his dreams many, many years later. I am grateful that I can share a fascination for psychology with my daughter, Wanda, who has sustained a keen interest in all my dream journeying. My niece Mikaela believed in this book as only a thirteen-year-old can and was the first to order a copy.

The close friendships with Anja, both Elke(s), Dagmar, Krista, Leo, Martin, Petra, and Sheila, (not all yet dream cherishers) were nurturing and much needed, particularly during occasional bouts of self-doubt. I also owe a lot to Brigit, my past love of many years, who supported me in many ways, including being my first dreamsensing 'guinea pig'. Yanny, my first love, has been a true, faithful and cherished companion on all my various journeys. A special additional thanks to my love, Barbara, who embodied completely the "supportive other" Rogers had in mind for encouraging a creative process and for so much more.

Last but certainly not least I thank my own dreaming world for keeping my passion alive and guiding me further. I am still not certain whether it really all comes from me, i.e., that all that I am dreaming is solely a product of my imagination. I have decided to stay open to the idea that other sources might sometimes link up with me during the night (and the day).

Introduction

Dreams and the Person-Centered Approach: Cherishing client experiencing – the title alone might give rise to some questions:

- Are there special person-centered ways to be with dreams?
- Are person-centered ways of being with dreams more helpful than other approaches?
- Why should person-centered practitioners cherish dreams? Isn't that out of their field of interest?
- "Cherish" – are dreams possibly more valuable than other issues?

And last but not least, we might also ask:

- What might Carl Rogers – the founder of the person-centered approach – say to all of this?

Given that dreams are at least important enough to have you pick up this book and find out more about them, you must have some hunch, however tentative, regarding the importance of dreams. Maybe a client came with, what was for her, a very significant dream and you felt you would have liked to have helped her more and ever since you have been wondering whether there is more to learn about dreams? Or perhaps you are a client, and you have had your share of therapists of different orientations, but none of these therapists have been helpful in understanding your dream life, and you want to know if a person-centered therapist might help. Or maybe there is a person-centered way to be with dreams *outside* of the therapeutic setting.

Many share an interest in finding out more about a person-centered way of being with dreams. Several person-centered theorists and practitioners write about dreams and their rich experiences of being with their clients and their dreams. However I can find only one book in German written about dreams, by Helga Lemke (2000), and only one book in English on Focusing and dreams, by Eugene Gendlin (1986). Clara Hill (1996, 2004) has written several books on her model of working with dreams, which I consider mainly person-centered and she terms cognitive-experiential.

It is my belief that the person-centered approach is one of the best ways of being with dreams, because it does not have any limiting concepts of dreaming or the meaning dreams bring with them. The person-centered approach puts the client's sense of her inner world at the center of the counseling work and gives primacy to the actualizing tendency (the inherent tendency of the organism to maintain and enhance itself – Mearns & Thorne, 2007). This suggests two ground rules for being with dreams: the dreamer finds her own meaning and dreaming is a process of self-healing.

The purpose of the first chapter is to give a theoretical underpinning to dreaming and of being with dreams in person-centered therapy. This includes understanding the dreaming process in and of itself within person-centered theory and pointing to the theoretical and practical significance of sharing dreams in therapy. The second chapter charts the territory of dreamsensing by viewing it as a creative endeavor and looking at the specific situations of the client and of the counselor. Concrete examples of dream sessions in Chapter 3 open up the possibility to experience three different pathways to understanding three dreams. These are the transcripts of dream sessions I had with

Helga Lemke (representing the "relational" person-centered way of being with dreams), Barbara McGavin (Focusing and dreamsensing) and Clara Hill (using a structural framework within her approach). While Chapter 3 includes looking at the dream sessions from the perspective of the client, Chapter 4 examines the role and aims of the therapists and further differentiates each of their approaches. Summing up with some concluding thoughts on the whole book, I have added appendices with further information. Appendix A: a short background overview of the person-centered approach and Focusing; Appendix B: biographical information on Lemke, McGavin, and Hill; Appendix C: a list of various resources for future contemplation of dreamsensing.

Finally, a brief explanation of my choice of some words. Searching for a good phrase to capture what happens when a client shares her dream with her counselor I eventually chose: "sensing into dreams" or "dreamsensing." In the literature the most frequently used term is "working with dreams" or "dreamwork." The term "work" leaves out the fun and free part of sensing into dreams, an activity that is both work and play. In German, Helga Lemke, coined the phrase "dream conversation" (*Traumgespräch*), which works especially well in the German context, where person-centered therapists call themselves *Gesprächstherapeuten*. However "conversation" seems to limit the dreamsensing to the talking cure and leaves out other creative methods such as art or body movement. "Sensing into a dream" also makes use of the double meaning of the word "sensing." It points to the use of all our bodily senses as well as to our capacity to "make sense," finding our own personal meaning of the dream. Dreamsensing has the additional advantage that it describes a process that one can do on one's own or together with someone else. Guiding someone through dreamsensing territory can be done as well outside of a formal therapy setting (e.g., in Focusing partnerships, or by medical doctors during a short consultation).

Since most clients and most therapists/counselors are female, this is the gender I use in my book – men are of course implied within the term. I use both therapy and counseling interchangeably, because the book pertains equally to both (and to more).

Cherishing has two meanings:

- To hold dear: treat with care and affection
- To keep deeply in mind (as a memory or purpose).

I want to take you along on a theoretical and practical journey, where hopefully at the end you will know why "cherishing" is just the right word when it comes to dreaming.

Situating Dreaming and Dreams in Person-Centered Theory and Practice

Person-centered theory that integrates dreaming is still at its beginning, even though Carl Rogers (1980, p. 314) explicitly called out for such a development. Since then several authors have written about the importance of dreams for therapy/counseling. In this first chapter I strive to show that a person-centered understanding of dreaming is to view it as a process of nightly self-healing, of nightly "psychological adjustment": the mainspring of dreaming being the actualizing tendency (similar to creative and therapeutic processes). Due to this significant role of dreaming and the fact that most people remember more dreams in times of transition and crisis – which are also the times when they seek out counselors or therapists – the art of sensing into dreams should be cultivated and taught more frequently within the person-centered world.

Rogers and dreams

Rogers begins the 19 propositions in his "Theory of Personality and Behavior" (1951) with the inner world of the client. This is both the starting point and a central part of his theory. Why then did he not mention the truly subjective process of the individual, which takes place every night – the dreaming experience? Why apparently concentrate solely on the waking world of the client? In *A Way of Being*, written almost 30 years later, Rogers calls upon "innovative educators and learners ... [to] have the courage, the creativity, and the skill to enter and learn this world of inner space" (1980, p. 314), and here he explicitly incorporates dreams as part of this inner space. In describing a fully functioning person, Rogers includes awareness of dreams as one important aspect: "Such a person is more potentially aware, not only of the stimuli from outside, but of ideas and dreams, and of the ongoing flow of feelings, emotions, and physiological reactions that he or she senses from within" (1980, p. 123). Rogers also mentions recording his own dreams (1980, p. 96).

Since then several person-centered authors have written about the importance of dreams (Conradi, 2000; Finke, 1990, 2004; Gerl, 1981; Hill, 2004; Jennings, 1986, 1995; Keil, 2002; Klingenbeck, 1998; Koch, 2009a; Lemke, 2000; Pfeiffer, 1989; Schmid, 1992; Vossen, 1990; Wijngaarden, 1991). Gendlin (1986) gave dreams a prominent role in Focusing with his book *Let Your Body Interpret Your Dreams*. The question of dreams has certain parallels with the question of the relevance of the body within person-centered theory and practice (Korbei, 2002; Teichmann-Wirth, 2002). Both areas are held "alive" within the person-centered community through the continuing influence of Focusing. Yet in recent publications where the relevance of the body at least has been integrated into the theory, dreams are still missing completely (Barrett-Lennard, 2003; Mearns & Cooper, 2005; Mearns & Thorne, 2007; Tudor & Worrall, 2006).

Several reasons can be found for why Rogers at first did not consider dreams as particularly relevant, and some of these factors continue to exert an influence.

- In 1951 the scientific research on dreams was still scant and not much was known about what actually happens while we are sleeping, including dreaming. "Not long ago, the very idea of 'brain activity in sleep' was thought to be an oxymoron. In fact, in the years following its discovery, REM sleep was often termed 'paradoxical' sleep, because the presence of waking-like EEG seemed so incongruous with the longstanding intuition that sleep was most fundamentally a state of inactivity" (Wamsley & Antrobus, 2007, p. 174).

- Rogers made it clear that person-centered therapy is distinct from psychoanalysis. It seems likely then that he accepted some of the psychoanalytical thinking about dreams and in effect distanced himself from dreams because of this. This included the beliefs that dreams are by definition unconscious processes and may only be understood by deep probing therein and only through interpretation by the psychoanalytical "expert." This equation of dreams with the unconscious can still be found in more recent person-centered literature (for example, see Thorne, 2003), even though dreams that are remembered are obviously part of our conscious awareness.

- Person-centered research and literature has mainly paid attention to the therapist's role. Mearns and Cooper: "Indeed it is paradoxical that *client-centred* therapy has, in its research and writing, focused so much on the work of the therapist. ... In fact, Rogers acknowledged this in a letter to Dave Mearns dated 4 January 1987, exactly one month before his death, stating, 'we have spent so much time looking at the part played by the therapist, and not enough at the part played by the client'" (2005, p. 44). Some research which did focus more on the client's part of the process did not include dreams: namely the client as an active self-healer (Bohart & Tallman, 1999) and the client's development of self-empathy (Barrett-Lennard, 2003).

- The focus of person-centered research and literature is more on the therapeutic relationship as the central healing factor, less on what happens within and with the client outside of the therapy context.

- Finally, the person-centered focus is on the development of the self and much less on the organism (including its body and dream worlds). "Despite its origins in organismic psychology, within person-centered psychology in general much more has been written about the self than the organism" (Tudor & Worrall, 2006, p. 102).

On the other hand, the emergence in the 1980s of the above-mentioned person-centered literature on dreams may be due to two trends on a more general level (notwithstanding Rogers' wish for more research on the "inner space"). During this time there was firstly an increase in interest in working with dreams within various psychotherapeutic schools of thought (Hill & Spangler, 2007). Secondly, the development of person-centered theory received a new boost: "It is a salutary note that theory development effectively stopped in the early 1960s in the discipline of client-centred therapy until after Rogers' death in the mid-80s" (Sanders & Wyatt, 2002, p. 16; see also Mearns, 1997, p. 128).

Coming to a contemporary person-centered theory on dreaming

The role of the actualizing tendency

Quite a few person-centered authors (Finke, 1990, 2004; Keil, 2002; Schmid, 1992; Vossen, 1990) agree that while dreaming, the actualizing tendency can express itself in a more primary or elemental way, and because of this dreams are of special interest for person-centered therapy processes:

> From a person-centered perspective the *phenomenon dream* is to be understood as an expression of the actualizing tendency. The basic tendency of the organism to develop and enhance its potentials is to be also seen as the initiator of the

psychological activities during sleep. The *concrete content of the dream* can be comprehended as the product of a conflict between the actualizing tendency and the self-actualizing tendency. ... in the dream the organismic actualizing tendency seems to get more of a chance to assert itself and resist the self-actualizing tendency. (Schmid, 1992, p. 392; my translation)

Dreams would therefore represent the result of the incongruence between self-concept and organismic perception. They have the function of illustrating – and therefore enabling expression of – tendencies that are not symbolized in waking consciousness. ... Aspects of this organismic tendency that have not yet been symbolized, a willingness to act that has not yet been perceived, could thus be integrated into the self-concept. (Finke, 1990, p. 505)

Schmid (1992) names two aspects of dreaming that enable the actualizing tendency to assert itself more: the partial tuning out of the dreamer's waking reality (laws of time and space are different during dreaming) and a partial tuning out of the dreamer's waking value orientation.

Dreaming as a creative process with a language of its own

Rogers' (1961, pp. 353–359) description of the creative process and his naming of the inner and outer conditions for fostering creativity can be very insightful when considering the dreaming process. The two outer conditions of "psychological safety" and "psychological freedom" as well as the three inner conditions of an "openness to experience," an "internal locus of evaluation" and an "ability to toy with elements and concepts" can be seen to be especially present during dreaming. While dreaming, dreamers often experience unusual and new ways of being; they

5

are not confronted with the direct value judgments of others, and the content of the dreams are often very original and playful combinations of experiences. Schmid states in a very similar way to Jung (1916/1990) before him: "Dreaming is always a creative event: the dreamer is author, director, stage designer, spectator of his dream, often also participating" (1992, p. 397, my translation). Schmid depicts dreams as being an encounter group with oneself.

Blechner evokes this creative dreaming process eloquently:

> … at night, life is different. We close our eyes, shut off our ears, and descend into a realm of existence where we are alone. For eight or so hours, we are freed from the constraints of functioning in a social world. For those precious hours, our minds are free to think about anything without worrying about being understood or judged. Released from the constraints of understandability and reality, we can think up new words, objects, and people, and we can create new situations. We are at the frontier of human experience. (2001, p. 3)

Due to the fact that we are communicating solely with ourselves, the creative language of our dreams has its very own logic and is often – when looked at from a waking perspective – a foreign language, or as Fromm (1951) called it "the forgotten language." Fromm explains the inner logic of dreams as follows:

> Mental activity during sleep has a logic different from that of waking existence. Sleep experience need not pay any attention to qualities that matter only when one copes with reality. … Sleep experience is not lacking in logic but is subject to different logical rules, which are entirely valid in that particular experiential state. … Waking life is taken up with the function of action, sleep is freed from it. Sleep is taken up with the function of self-experience. (1951, p. 28)

Gendlin states: "The dream does not hide its 'message in metaphorical code.' The dream is born metaphorically" (1986, p. 150). Or as Hill puts it: "The language of dreaming seems to make use of two essentially human communication characteristics: the use of metaphors and our propensity to tell stories" (1996, p. 48).

Dreaming as a process of nightly healing similar to the therapeutic process

According to Rogers (1961, p. 350) the "mainspring" of creativity seems to be the actualizing tendency, the same "curative force" (ibid.) active in psychotherapy and I would add also the mainspring of dreams. In this way, I would answer Rogers' question: "Is it possible for the whole body, the whole organism, to learn something that the mind does not know, or only learns later?" (1980, p. 312) by stating: "Yes, every night while we are dreaming." I would propose – and attempt to show in the following – that while dreaming the whole organism is not only striving to become more congruent and wise, it is undergoing a process of self-healing similar in direction to the processes of healing which occur during therapy.

At this point it is important to remember that our conscious knowing about the dream experience is by definition finite: we cannot at the same time dream and communicate in a waking conscious state. Rogers describes a similar problem when trying to put the creative process into words: "But we cannot expect an accurate description of the creative act, for by its very nature it is indescribable. This is the unknown which we must recognize as unknowable until it occurs" (1961, p. 355). Our waking consciousness, including the structures of our thinking, has a considerable impact on what we remember of our dreaming experiences of the night. Freud's idea that not every person dreams every night is based on the belief that dream experience and dream memory are the same. Research on dreams has since proven that we all dream regularly throughout the night, even if we don't remember any dreams (Barrett & McNamara, 2007). The nightly dream experiencing seems to be much richer and more complex than what is usually remembered of it.

Are there curative experiences outside of therapy and outside of the relationship?

Rogers points to possible curative experiences outside of the therapy room in his "Theory of Personality and Behavior":

> ... the acceptance of experiences inconsistent with the self often occurs between interviews, without ever being verbalized to the counselor. The essential factor appears to be that the person achieves the attitude that it is safe to look at organic experience and then can permit it to be symbolized in consciousness even though the therapist is not present. (1951, p. 518)

Rogers goes on to say that an individual can face these inconsistent experiences alone if they are not deeply denied.

Rogers seems to have changed his view several times on how important being in a relationship is for significant therapeutic change to occur. In 1957, in his famous article "The Necessary and Sufficient Conditions of Therapeutic Personality Change" he states: "I am hypothesizing that *significant* positive personality change *does not occur except* in a relationship. This is of course a hypothesis, and it may be disproved" (1957/1989, p. 221, emphasis added). Tudor and Worrall (2006, p. 192) specifically address this issue: "Rogers' inclusion of psychological contact as a *necessary* condition raises a question for us: is a relationship between two people really necessary for therapeutic change to occur?" Tudor and Worrall come to the conclusion that Rogers omits the first condition of psychological contact in a chapter published after his death (see Rogers &

Sanford, 1989) because Rogers saw that being in a relationship was not the only way.

> Although many people experience moments of change within the immediacy of a relationship, there seems no reason why those moments should necessarily occur *only* in relationship. To return to our electrical analogy: there are some tasks that require electricity, and some that we can achieve more efficiently or effectively with electricity. Electricity, however is not the only source of power, and some of us, sometimes cook with gas. (Tudor & Worrall, 2006, p. 193)

If we take as a given the statement of Rogers, that the individual can face inconsistent experiences *alone*, the essential factor for the learning process "perhaps the most important learning of which a person is capable, namely the learning of self" (1951, p. 519) is that the "person achieves the attitude that it is *safe* to look" (p. 518, emphasis added). Is the dream not often such a personal place, where it is seemingly safe to experience a variety of possibilities, to expand the awareness of that which can be permitted into consciousness in waking life?

Dreaming could then be a process of nightly self-healing, of "psychological adjustment" a "reorganization of the structure of self" through a "self-initiated apprehension of the new material" (Rogers, 1951, proposition XV, pp. 513–515). Dreaming can be understood as a process striving to integrate in an internally consistent way all the sensory and visceral experiences on a symbolic level into the concept of self. "Once this type of integration occurs, then the tendency toward growth can become fully operative, and the individual moves in directions normal to all organic life" (p. 514). Rogers explicitly states that in order for this integration process to happen, it does not have to happen consciously, the experiences do not necessarily have to be present in consciousness. This would cover the fact that the greatest part of dreams are not ever present in waking consciousness (even though they are potentially available, if the dreamer is, for instance, woken up) but still could have the function of psychological adjustment. Rogers correlates such an integration with "freedom from inner tension" (p. 513) which is something people may feel while they are dreaming (nightmares being an example of the opposite effect, a possible sign that the integration process has come to a halt).

Rogers goes on to state that the function of conscious acceptance of impulses and perceptions is an increase of the possibilities of conscious control:

> ... I do not immediately gain my conscious objective, but by accepting all the evidences of experience and organizing them into one integrated perceptual system, I acquire the control by which reasonable conscious objectives can be achieved. This is very parallel to the feeling of the person who has completed therapy. (pp. 514–515)

This is a basic paradox Rogers often points to in his writings: by loosening my conscious control, by letting my self-concept become more fluid, more expansive, I gain a sense of control, a sense of autonomy, of self-government. So by giving ourselves over to sleep, letting our sense of awareness become more expansive during dreams, we strive to become a unified organism, seeking the most possible integration of our sensory and visceral experiences of the present, past, and future. As Rogers puts it so succinctly: "organisms are always seeking, always initiating, always 'up to something'" (1980, p. 123).

Rogers points to a trust in the wisdom of the organism as one of the significant elements of any helping relationship:

> a trust in the *"wisdom of the organism"* to lead us to the core of her problem. ... But when trusted, her organism, her

nonconscious mind – call it what you will – can follow the path that leads to crucial issues. ... I want to make it possible for my client to move in her own way, and at her own pace, to the heart of her conflicts. ... Perhaps pointing out these elements will have made it clear that a person-centered approach in therapy leads to a very subtle, often intricate process, *a process that has an organic flow of its own.* (1986/ 1989, p. 151, emphasis added)

So a trust in the nonconscious mind, the wisdom of the organism which leads us to the crucial events, is essential for the person-centered therapist (and is also one of the important "lessons" the client learns through therapy). *This can be seen as a description of what happens during our dreaming: the wisdom of the organism leading us to the crucial issues in our lives, with an "organic flow of its own," helping us in our task of integrating experiences and self-concept and letting the actualizing tendency come to its fullest potential.*

Dreaming can enhance self-empathy and interpersonal empathy

Another aspect that arises while contemplating the similarities of the processes of dreaming and therapy is the empathic functioning of the *client* during therapy. Barrett-Lennard draws attention to this function of empathy when he links the development of self-empathy with the development of interpersonal empathy: "Thus it can be said that self-empathy opens the way to interpersonal empathy. Deep empathic engagement with others probably also fosters self-empathy" (2003, p. 48). Barrett-Lennard calls interpersonal and self-empathy a "twin phenomenon" that is not identical but closely interdependent. In this sense, the potentially self-empathic process of dreaming also enhances the interpersonal empathy during counseling and vice versa, one might even say they are interdependent.

One common example of the possible interdependence of the dreaming process and the change process stimulated by therapy would be recurring dreams that stop. Finding an understanding of the dream during therapy would be one way for the disappearance of the recurring dream to occur. Another equally viable way would be when the therapy process has stimulated a change in issues linked with the recurrent dreams and the dreaming process changes in accordance with this. If we view this on a continuum of a meaning-creating process of dreaming, waking, remembering some dreams, talking about dreams within the context of therapy for example, we see these processes as going in the same healing direction, through enhancing the self-empathy and the self-healing potentials of the client-dreamer.

To appreciate the dreams of a client then is to come two steps closer to the client's perspective. One step is through attending to dreams, to what happens in between the therapeutic sessions in the inner world of the client. The other step would be by seeing how the client's dreams can play an important part in leading the way, in pointing to the core of her problems. In this sense both steps help the therapist to stay truly "client-centered" in content and process.

A great part of dreaming is not remembered in conscious waking life and yet we can reason that dreaming has its own generally healing effect on the ongoing processes of the organism, resulting in more congruence. Staying with Rogers' above-mentioned differentiation (that an individual can face experiences inconsistent with the self if they are not deeply denied), we can postulate that there will be dreams that process experiences or complexes of experiences so threatening to the self-concept ("deep denial") that they need the caring and empathic presence of another to be integrated. Certain types of dreams, such as nightmares or anxiety dreams, might be an example of this kind of a process. On the other hand, there will be dreams, many of which are not remembered, that lead to psychological adjustment and integration of experiences which are not threatening. In a similar way Finke states: "The urge to become whole, i.e., to complete the design, is fulfilled in dreams" (1990, p. 506). Vossen (1990), Finke (1990) and Schmid (1992) see dreaming as a sort of "test behavior" in which dreams are "one step ahead of our consciousness and of our conscious actions" (Vossen, 1990, p. 542).

Focusing and dreaming

Gendlin (1986, 1996) has a somewhat different concept of the process of dreaming. He sees dreams as "unfinished events" in contrast to a felt sense, which is a "more than finished event" (1986, p. 154). Dreams might reveal the next step but Focusing is needed to find and to realize the next growth step.

> Except in rare cases, the step forward is not actually in the dream. It comes from the energy that the dream's images imply and create. … *What is next is only what the client's body makes of the dream.* (1996, p. 200)

Gendlin seems to have come a long way in his conceptualization of dreams. According to Keil (2002), in the 1960s, Gendlin originally thought that dreams were not relevant for therapy. Even though Gendlin dramatically changed his opinion of the therapeutic value of dreams, eventually seeing them as important, he held on to the idea that therapeutic steps come *from* dreams and not *in* dreams.

> In deeply relaxed states we do not fully appreciate what comes. In a dream we rarely know it is a dream. The body-sense that interprets everything has been relaxed. The whole way we are is not fully ongoing, so all of it cannot respond. … We cannot "integrate" what is new when we are in the dream… (Gendlin, 1986, p. 159)

One might hypothethize that Gendlin based his theory on those dream experiences which are usually remembered, those which stay with us and might "need" more waking understanding (e.g., nightmares). However, there is also ample literature on other types of dreams (Krippner, Bogzaran, & Carvalho, 2002; Siegel, 2002; Taylor, 1992). In their book *Extraordinary Dreams and How to Work with Them*, Krippner, Bogzaran, and Carvalho (2002) mention several types of dreams, where one would have to say the step forward came in the dream (e.g., creative dreams, lucid dreams, healing dreams, telepathic dreams, precognitive dreams, and spiritual dreams). Another example would be a series of dreams in which eventually the issue is resolved and cleared all within the dreaming process – without any Focusing happening.

This is where we come to the limits of our understanding mentioned earlier, the point at which "we must recognize the unknowable" (Rogers, 1961, p. 355). Yet how the dreaming process is conceptualized has a definite impact on how we approach the dream narration. Gendlin's view places the power of change primarily within the Focusing process. Thus for him, dreaming is of secondary importance, in that it brings up vital issues that the dreamer should focus on, but is not itself the immediate vehicle of change. If, on the other hand, dreaming is seen as a self-healing process as suggested earlier, similar in direction to therapy, then the process of dreaming is in and of itself vital for the person. The self-healing process of dreams can be enhanced and strengthened by further waking understanding, e.g., through counseling, or Focusing by oneself.

I would go one step further and suggest that dreaming is not only a process similar to therapy, it is also similar to Focusing, in the sense that Focusing is a "process of developing more congruent symbols for organismic experiencing" (Iberg, 1996, p. 32). Both dreaming and Focusing are experienced immediately and in a bodily way – even if the body is in a different process state during waking and sleeping. Whilst I agree with Gendlin that the "body-sense that interprets everything" (1986, p. 159) is relaxed during dreaming, that does not mean that it is not functioning in a meaningful way. As far as I can ascertain, no one has considered the similarities between the processes of Focusing and dreaming. Weiser Cornell (2005) mentions that for a full felt sense to develop during Focusing, four aspects are important: body sensations, emotional quality, imagery or symbolism, and life connection or story. All these aspects are predominant during dreaming. Staying in the Focusing language, felt shifts also definitely happen while dreaming; we can find them not only in dream narratives but also in the physiological shifts and body changes that take place while dreaming. In this sense I would like to suggest that *dreaming might be conceived of as a process of "multidimensional fast-motion Focusing"* or Focusing as a process of slow-motion dreaming.

Some remaining theoretical questions

At present I see two differing conceptions of the dreaming process within person-centered and experiential psychotherapies and counseling. This is in contrast to Keil (2002), who, in a review of the then current person-centered literature on dreams, differentiates three concepts of dreams. Keil cites Schmid (1992) as placing the dream experience within the state of disorganization (as Rogers described in his theory of personality); Vossen (1988) and Finke (1994) as standing for the view that in dreams the actualizing tendency can express itself in a most original way; and Gendlin's conception that dreams are unfinished experiences needing Focusing to move forward. Whereas I agree with Keil's assertion that Gendlin's conception differs from the others, I disagree with his further distinction between Schmid and Finke. Finke (1990) and Schmid (1992) have a very similar view. Keil (2002) does not sufficiently take into account that Schmid (1992) only places dreams in the area of disorganized behavior in a context where he specifically describes anxiety dreams and not the dreaming process in general. Schmid (1992) states that a dream is a congruent expression of the person (experiencing and symbolization), and because of this, incongruence (experience and self) is seen more clearly.

Notwithstanding these two conceptions of dreaming, a person-centered theory of the dreaming process is still in its infancy. It has to further integrate a process view of dreaming and substantiate its interdependence with the counseling process (although first steps have been taken by Finke, 1990, 2004; Hill, 2004; Koch, 2009b; Lemke, 2000; Schmid, 1992). It would be interesting to research the extent to which the evolution of a client's dreaming process parallels her therapy process; comparing the evolution of dreams in therapies with varying (positive and negative) outcomes. Further differentiation is needed along the continuum of differing types of dreaming processes (see Hill, 2004; Lemke, 2000). Research on dreams could yield more insight into the healing processes that happen outside of therapy, giving the self-healing potential of the client a more central place.

Another issue awaiting further clarification is the relationship between dream-experience/dream-narrative and consciousness or what comes into awareness and what does not – during dreaming and upon waking – and how this is related to the ongoing valuing process. Lucid dreaming – when the dreamer knows she is dreaming while dreaming and can influence her dreaming process in a more active way – is a particular dreaming experience that needs to be considered in more detail when considering these issues. Another special dreaming experience is having pre-cognitive dreams. Integral to these questions are the concepts of "consciousness," "awareness," "symbolization," "non-consciousness," "subception," and "perception" within the person-centered theoretical framework (see Coulson, 2000; Ellingham, 2002; Purton, 2004).

The significance of sharing dreams within therapy

Interdependent meaning-creating processes

When considering the importance of sharing dreams within therapy, it is important to consider the role that dreaming has within our ongoing meaning-creating processes. There is an interdependent and cyclical weaving process happening both during waking and dreaming hours. If we start looking at the meaning-creating process by considering the dreaming experience itself, we can notice a shift in the meaning-creating once we wake up. Our waking capabilities will limit what of the dreaming process we will remember and be able to symbolize, thus the dreaming experience becomes a dream memory. When we share the dream with someone else, it becomes a narrative, and a further shift in meaning happens — due to the presence of an other we might remember more or reveal less. This sharing is similar to the dreaming process itself: a meaning-creating process with an organic flow of its own. At each bend in the journey, meaning might be lost or gained and will eventually blend and change once more in the nightly dreaming process that follows.

When the process dimension of dreaming is considered in this way, it becomes harder to view a dream as an "unfinished" or "finished" event, or like a "piece of art" (Schmid, 1992, p. 397), where "freshness" (Jennings, 1986, p. 316) is essential, or has a certain "contradictory and problematic structure" including the "importance of the beginning" (Vossen, 1990, p. 518). When viewed as a meaning-creating process, the statement "the dream is the dream is the dream" (Jennings, 1986, p. 310) becomes misleading; closer to the truth would be: dreaming becomes a dream memory, becomes a dream narrative, weaves into a dream conversation, becomes dreaming …. As Gendlin states in his most recent article on dreams: "Dreaming is a living process, not just frozen pictures. When we let the pictures bring their bodily quality, dreamwork continues the living process" (2012, in press).

17

Dreaming is a process that occurs nightly, therapy maybe weekly, and both activate the self-healing potential of the client. When dreaming and therapy are seen as interdependent meaning-making processes it becomes clear that they can enhance and support each other.

In a similar vein, Bohart conceptualizes how change in therapy works:

> It's clients who make therapy work through the human capacities for self-healing and self-righting. However, we do not really know how the process works. I suggest that much of the process is nonconscious. It involves moving from a state of defensiveness, hypervigilence, or hopelessness to a state of active, receptive openness. A state of active receptive openness promotes clients' noticing new possibilities both inside and outside therapy, trying new things out, and having new creative insights and ideas "bubble up." Many changes that occur may happen nonconsciously. Any experience that promotes an organismic openness to learning will increase the chances of positive change happening. (2008, p. 185)

While there are differences in how the dreaming process in itself is conceptualized, many authors agree that dream narratives and sharing and working with them (i.e., having "dream conversations" = *Traumgespräche*) can be of considerable significance to the therapeutic process; they can make a "remarkable and unique contribution ... in each individual's quest for meaning and self understanding" (Jennings, 1986, p. 332). Dream narratives are cherished for their "heightened emotional quality" (ibid., p. 312); for being of additional value for self-experiencing and showing "unused possibilities" (Schmid, 1992, p. 399); for revealing "the intricacies of our current lives" (Gendlin, 1986, p. 157); for being "related to his or her waking hours" and providing "insights into his or her 'inner world'" (Finke, 1990, p. 504); for being "rich, condensed, *special sources of experience* with a very specific dynamic power, with their own possibilities" (Vossen, 1990, p. 523).

Research has shown that dream experiencing is especially intense during life situations where persons are more prone to seek counseling or therapeutic help, i.e., in times of crisis and upheaval. "There is a dramatic upsurge in the number and intensity of dreams at life crises and transitions. Even the physiological experience of dreaming undergoes a transformation" (Siegel, 2002, p. 17). There are "typical" dream issues that persons dream while being pregnant, or while going through divorce (Siegel, 2002), as well as certain "types" of dreams preparing for death (Bulkeley & Bulkley, 2005) or accompanying a grieving process (Hess, 2004; Siegel, 2002). Nightmares that come after traumatic events are a very common and relatively well-researched phenomenon (Hartmann, 2001; Heaton, 2004; Siegel, 2002). Lemke (2000) argues that such impressive dreams are demanding to be told.

Hill notes that certain types of dreams require attention in therapy because they seem to reflect issues that need to be dealt with: "particularly vivid or salient dreams, troubling dreams, recurrent dreams, nightmares, or sleep terrors" (1996, p. 59). Reviewing the research on dreams and psychotherapy, Hill and Spangler come to the conclusion that: "there is strong evidence that working with dreams therapeutically is useful. If we can use dreams to increase self-understanding and if we can make changes in problems that are troubling us after working with dreams, these are compelling reasons for paying attention to dreams" (2007, p. 179). Gendlin states: "Dreams are an irreplaceable avenue of therapy for two reasons: (1) what is far from the client's awareness cannot be processed, but if it comes up in a dream, it can immediately be processed; (2) dreams translate a person's problem into images that implicitly contain an energy that moves toward a solution" (1996, p. 199).

Five approaches to being with dreams

In the last thirty years five different approaches to being with dreams have developed within the person-centered community:

- Working with dreams in a "relational" person-centered way, where ensuring a high-quality therapeutic relationship is the essential guiding principle of the dream session (see Schmid, 1992; Lemke, 2000).
- Structural dreamwork: Different phases or stages structure the dream session. This includes offering certain specific exercises in working with the dream (see Finke, 1990, 2004; Hill, 1996, 2004).
- Dreams and Focusing (see Dawson, 2000; Gendlin, 1986, 1992, 1996, 2012; Graessner, 1989; Leijssen, 2004).
- Dream chronological approach (see Jennings, 1986; Vossen, 1990).
- "Traditional" person-centered dream conversations about the current emotional meanings connected with the dream, without further consideration of the content of the dream.

I would consider especially the first three approaches viable person-centered ways of sensing into dreams (see Chapters 3 and 4 for a more detailed description of each). Which approach is used depends mostly on the personal needs and preferences of the client and the therapist.

Jennings and Vossen differ from the first two approaches in a way that seems to me to be problematic. They both place a lot of emphasis on following the dream chronology and keeping the client "on track." Vossen describes his way of working as follows:

> I also keep a very close eye on the *order* of everything, which appears to be extremely important, and on the function of

the image as a whole. Therefore people often think I am a fusspot, tough and persevering but, later, they are thankful because it was through this they gained access to a concealed and impenetrable aspect of themselves which would otherwise have been lost to them. ... Naturally, this method encounters more resistance than Gendlin's method, but one continually breaks through all the things the client fails to notice, neglects or avoids. (1990, pp. 532–533)

The danger I see here is that the therapist has a fixed concept of what is most important in a dream and which exact path to follow and becomes too directive in content and process, limiting the client's freedom to "lead the way" (see also Chapter 2 for a thorough discussion of such "danger zones").

The last approach I termed the "traditional" person-centered way, concentrates mainly on the current emotional meaning the dream carries and not on the content of the dream (see Stumm, 1992). In this way it misses out on the essential gifts, the richness and creativity the dream story can bring.

Three central assumptions

In person-centered literature on working with dreams all authors share three basic assumptions. All three assumptions differ explicitly from the traditional psychoanalytical way of working with dreams.

1. The client is the expert in understanding her dream. Only she can sense into and decide if a found meaning of the dream, or a dream segment, is plausible or feels right.
2. This defines the role of the therapist or counselor as being a stimulant for, or companion in the client's meaning-creating process and not being the interpreter. The counselor's or therapist's role is a supportive not a directive one.

3. Dreams do not hide or disguise their message. They come to us in their own inherent form of language, which might be foreign to the waking consciousness.

Obstacles to working with dreams in the person-centered community

One of the obstacles encountered on the person-centered "royal road" to organismic experiencing through dream sharing is a general devaluation of dreaming and dreams. We can see certain parallels between how dreams are valued on the level of person-centered theory, person-centered counselors, clients, and society as a whole. On the personal level dreams are often "ignored because there is no perceived relationship to the self-structure" (Rogers, 1951, p. 503) and not "owned," not felt to be part of the self (ibid., pp. 509–510). When viewed on the level of person-centered theory it seems that dream experiencing has been mostly ignored and this appears to hold true at the level of society also, at least when considering mainstream Western culture. In this sense our culture does not view dreams as part of its conscious self; they are neither part of the "self-concept" of society, nor are they integrated into society's "self-structure." Clients and counselors work within – and are influenced by – this societal and theoretical context.

Personal attitudes toward dreams can of course be very ambivalent. On the one hand, dreams seem to be important, they sometimes wake us up, and they cling to us in waking life. On the other hand, they are hard to grasp, memory fails us again and again, or we are confronted with very strange leftovers. Some dreams are experienced as very frightening, and they engage us tremendously, so much so we seem to be stuck with them – sometimes for years – even though we might like to forget them as fast as we forget all our other dreams. Generally, there are very few people around us who at that moment say: "This is important, let's share this, talking about it will strengthen your tendency to actualize, maintain and enhance your experiencing organism"!

If I as a client had a dream that was puzzling, even frightening, would I be inclined to go to a therapist who cherishes dreams, who knows what the potential of dreams can be, and who has experience in accompanying people on their travels through the dream world? If I have a nightmare or a repetitive dream sequence, the dream world is telling me this is important, my valuing may be ambivalent but the experience is very real, very there, very pushy. Still, deciding to share it with someone is for some people a big step. If the therapist doesn't support this step to the same degree that she supports other experiences of the client such as feelings and felt senses, the therapist will not be the midwife she is supposed to be. ("The therapist becomes the 'midwife' of change, not its originator" Rogers, 1977, p. 15.)

Another obstacle is encountered at the beginning of a therapy process. Empirical studies have shown that different valuing of dreams on the part of the therapist correlates with the amount of dreams brought into therapy (Hill, 2004; Schredl, Bohusch, Kahl, Mader & Somesan, 2000; Stolte & Koch, 1992). Yet most person-centered therapists will probably wait until the client has built up enough trust to begin giving us a glimpse of what is going on in her night world (see Stumm, 1992). Is this what is meant by being nondirective – don't "prescribe" the content of the session, do not be judgmental about what the client brings with her, do not value one content above the other? Are dreams a "content" or are dreams part of everyday life, a forgotten or forsaken part that has to be asked for, before it is appreciated, shared? We could ask at the beginning of a session, "What have you brought from your night and day experiencing, since we saw each other last?" That would really be nonjudgmental, accepting and nondirective, inclusive of *all* experience, not valuing one above another (not, for example, valuing waking life above dreaming life).

Giving dreams a significant place in theory, practice and training

When it is clear in the person-centered world that dreams have an important place both theoretically and practically, then it will also be obvious to the client as well that her dreams will be valued. The client would know that she can bring a dream to the counseling session and that this will be welcomed, and she will feel that it is an appropriate place to talk about it. However, at the present time, if she goes to a person-centered therapist, she may sadly more often than not, experience no such dream-welcoming climate. Some person-centered therapists may at present integrate dreams into their personal theoretical and practical concepts, without any further development of theory, but they will do this often with a feeling of trepidation, as if they weren't being congruent within their person-centered approach (see Conradi, 2000; Klingenbeck, 1998). This undervaluing of a key aspect of a client's experiencing will continue unless the foundation within person-centered theory integrates dreams more explicitly and, in doing so, also makes a concerted effort to give dreams and dreamsensing a more central place in the training and education of counselors and therapists.

Summary of the main points

- Within the dreaming process the actualizing tendency can express itself in a more original way.

- Dreaming is a process of self-healing, or psychological adjustment; a process where the organism is striving to integrate in an internally consistent way all the sensory and visceral experiences of the past, present and future.

- While dreaming, as in therapy, the wisdom of the organism is leading us to the crucial issues in our lives, and doing so with an organic flow of its own.

- The development of self-empathy enhances interpersonal empathy. Dreaming is a process of strengthening self-empathy and as such can enhance the interpersonal empathy being developed within and outside of the therapeutic process.

- The dreaming process of the client is a self-healing process that occurs outside of therapy. When explicitly integrated into therapy, dreams not only can lead to the crucial issues in the client's life, but they can also give insights about the changes happening stimulated by the therapeutic process. To appreciate the dreams of a client, then, is to come two steps closer to the client's perspective.

- There is an ongoing meaning-creating process, interweaving dreaming and waking life. The dreaming experience becomes a dream memory, changes into a dream narrative, evolves through sharing the dream with a counselor, and weaves into the following dreaming experience ...

- Focusing and dreaming can be understood as similar processes in the sense that both develop more congruent symbols for organismic experiencing. One can conceive of dreaming as a process of multidimensional fast-motion Focusing.

- In times of crisis and transition more dreams are remembered and want to be told and understood. This makes it essential for therapists to explicitly state from the beginning of therapy that the client's sharing of dreams is valued. In this way, clients willing to work with dreams, or being troubled by dreams will be ensured that they have the needed support of the therapist.

- Three basic assumptions guide the person-centered way of sensing into dreams: (a) the dreamer is the expert in understanding her dream, (b) the counselor is a stimulant for the meaning-creating process of the dream not its interpreter, (c) the dream does not disguise or cover up its meaning.

- The attitudes toward dreaming within the general cultural environment, as well as within the client's and the therapist's personal environment, can have a significant influence on remembering or wanting to share dreams. This is why dreams need "affirmative action" within person-centered theory, training and therapy.

2

Sensing into Dreams: Charting the territory

In the first chapter I used Rogers' (1961) description of the creative process to help us understand the dreaming process. In this chapter I expand further on this idea by considering dreamsensing within therapy as a creative process. In particular Rogers' ideas about the inner and outer conditions that foster the creative process and its concomitants can illuminate the territory of dreamsensing within a therapeutic setting. After this general dreamsensing "map," I will set out what is special about the client's situation when she shares her dream. I then examine the coordinates of the therapist's role, including her own process as well as the therapeutic process.

Rogers' description of the creative process

> My definition, then, of the creative process is that it is the emergence in action of a novel relational product, growing out of the uniqueness of the individual on the one hand, and the materials, events, people, or circumstances of his life on the other. (1961, p. 350)

While sensing into dreams client and counselor join together on a creative journey "bringing back" new experiences, insights and meaning. Rogers' conditions for the fostering of the creative process are essential to the value and success of this dreamsensing expedition.

Rogers mentions three significant *inner conditions* that must be permitted to emerge:

- *Openness to experience*: "means lack of rigidity and permeability of boundaries in concepts, beliefs, perceptions and hypotheses. It means a tolerance for ambiguity where ambiguity exists. It means the ability to receive conflicting information without forcing closure upon the situation" (1961, pp. 353–354).

- *An internal locus of evaluation*: Rogers points to internalizing the source of evaluative judgment as perhaps the most fundamental condition. "Have I created something satisfying to *me* – my feeling or my thought, my pain or my ecstasy?" (p. 354).

- *The ability to toy or play with elements and concepts*: "It is from this spontaneous toying and exploration that there arises the hunch, the creative seeing of life in a new and significant way" (p. 355).

Rogers' two *external conditions* that nourish the above internal conditions and foster creativity are:

- *Psychological safety*: Here Rogers points to three associated processes: (1) accepting the individual as of unconditional worth; (2) providing a climate in which external evaluation is absent; (3) understanding empathically.

- *Psychological freedom*: The therapist permits the client a complete freedom of symbolic expression. "This permissiveness gives the individual complete freedom to think, to feel, to be, whatever is most inward within himself" (1961, p. 358).

While sensing into dreams both the client and the counselor need to foster the three inner conditions within themselves. The counselor is the one responsible for ensuring and fostering the two outer conditions.

Rogers (1961, pp. 355–356) also names *four concomitants* to the creative act:

- Evidence of discipline, an attempt to bring out the essence
- Anxiety of separateness
- Desire to communicate
- Eureka feeling

While dreamsensing, these four aspects are especially present within a therapy session. The coming together of client and therapist is in and of itself an evidence of discipline, of a joint venture in trying to understand the deeper meaning of the dream. The anxiety of separateness is markedly present while sharing a dream. As Rogers puts it so nicely: "Persons begin revealing material that they have never communicated before, in the process of discovering previously unknown elements in themselves ... such discoveries are unsettling but exciting" (1980, p. 155). As I have pointed out in the first chapter, there are dreams that want to be told and want to be shared. Last but not least, once a dream has been understood, often a "eureka feeling," a surprise or an "aha" arises.

Delineating the client's space

When sharing a dream, a client ventures into *unknown territory*. She might be sharing something she has never shared before. Added to this, both she and her counselor will not know at the start of the journey where they will end up or what they will encounter on the way. More than with other issues brought into therapy sessions, *dreams can make the client feel especially vulnerable and in a way "blind."* This I find is due in part to four paradoxes that we are confronted with when sharing a dream:

1. The dreamer thinks she uncovers everything by sharing a dream, yet she actually uncovers very little.

2. The dream is dreamt by the dreamer, only she can recall it, yet it is often not felt as if it is of her own making. Sometimes it even feels as if she is being lived by the dream.

3. She dreams in her own unique language, yet often has no understanding of it.

4. We are on our own in our dreaming world, yet the understanding of this world is often easier in the company of another.

This potential "blindness" of the client to the meaning of her dreams can also be accentuated by other factors such as the client's inexperience with sharing dreams and finding their creative and rich meanings. Closely related to this is the devaluation of dreaming, (mentioned in Chapter 1), which we generally encounter in Western societies and thus might also find in the personal environment of the client. Lastly there is the question of what happens in the first waking appraisal by the dreamer of a particular dream. Even among dream enthusiasts one can find a special valuing of certain types of dreams above others, e.g., a devaluing of everyday "mundane" dreams. This kind of "waking-life logic" dismisses certain dreams as senseless or worthless. Also, a "waking-life resistance" to whatever issues the dream is touching upon can influence this value judgment. Such incongruence between experiencing and awareness can elicit a need to defend against the seemingly threatening or "mundane" aspects of the dream.

Due to this potential "blindness" and inexperience a special vulnerability emerges when the client begins to share her dreams, making it essential to foster the inner conditions and ensuring the outer conditions that Rogers specifies for the creative process. An *opening up to experience* occurs once the client begins sharing her dreams and becomes acquainted with her particular dream world. If there is no inner sense of what she is revealing, this might be a very scary step to take. The "blindness" involved in this process requires *an inner compass to lead the way*, her inner locus of evaluation. Only this can help her navigate within the meaning-creating process that ensues. Also significant while dreamsensing is a fostering of Rogers' third condition: *an ability "to play* spontaneously with ideas, ... relationships – ... to shape wild hypotheses, to make the given problematic, to express the ridiculous, to translate from one form to another" (Rogers, 1961, p. 355, emphasis added).

When venturing into this somewhat strange territory of the dream world, the discoveries can be "unsettling and exciting," as Rogers notes about the creative process. They can also stir up a very unwanted and painful emotion: *shame.* As Brown, who has done extensive research on this topic points out: "Shame is about the fear of disconnection. When we are experiencing shame, we are steeped in the fear of being ridiculed, diminished or seen as flawed. We are afraid that we've exposed or revealed a part of us that jeopardizes our connection and our worthiness of acceptance" (2007, p. 20). *Our propensity to avoid shame can have an influence on our willingness to share dreams or parts of dreams.* For some, admitting that dreams are troubling might already be shameful. Shame can arise due to the fact that in some dreams we are behaving in a way we would be "ashamed" of in waking life. In addition, when starting out on our dreamsensing journey we often don't have a clue as to what possibly shameful issues will "bubble up" due to the dream sharing. Gender might also influence how easy it is to share a dream. Brown concludes that men experience shame for different reasons than women.

How a client "moves" in this dreamsensing landscape will depend on her valuing of the dream she wants to share and on the quality of experience she brings with her in sensing into her dreams. A client coming with an awareness of how important the dreaming process is for her journey of self-discovery will share and sense into her dreams differently than a client who has disturbing nightmares she wants to get rid of. A client with no experience in dream sharing, or with hurtful past dream-sharing experiences, might feel more vulnerable and fearful than a client with extensive experience in dreamsensing.

The counselor's coordinates

Starting out

Getting a sense of where the client situates herself vis-à-vis her dreaming experiencing is an important step at the beginning of a counseling process. Some questions about the client might need an initial answer. How does the client value her dreams generally, and how might that relate to the one she is sharing in particular? How much experience does she have in dreamsensing? Does the client first need an input from the counselor's side as to why the counselor finds dreams worthy of attention? A clear theory of, and experience in, dreamsensing are prerequisites for the initial orientation of the client. I, as a counselor, might share with the client my ideas about how an appreciation of dreaming as a self-healing process can strengthen her sense of autonomy; I might also suggest that if she experiences her unique answers as coming from within – the nightly "spring" being already owned by her – she can gain a sense of her own inherent healing capacities. I might mention that sensing into her dreams can strengthen her curiosity about her inner world and give her a sense of wonder about the creative gifts of sleep. I might share my belief that dreamsensing is a creative process that enhances not only her self-empathy, but also her interpersonal empathy and in that way also strengthens the whole therapeutic process.

Accompanying the client

Rogers' description of an *empathic way of being with another person* can be used as a "blueprint" for how to accompany clients when they share their dreams.

> It means entering the private perceptual world of the other and becoming thoroughly at home in it. It involves being sensitive, moment by moment, to the changing felt meanings which flow in this other person, to the fear or rage or tenderness or confusion or whatever that he or she is experiencing. It means temporarily living in the other's life, moving about in it delicately without making judgments; it means sensing meanings of which he or she is scarcely aware, but not trying to uncover totally unconscious feelings, since this would be too threatening. It includes communicating your sensings of the person's world as you look with fresh and unfrightened eyes at the elements of which he or she is fearful. It means frequently checking with the person as to the accuracy of your sensings, and being guided by the responses you receive. You are a confident companion to the person in his or her inner world. By pointing to the possible meanings in the flow of another person's experiencing, you help the other to focus on this useful type of referent, to experience the meanings more fully, and to move forward in the experiencing. To be with another in this way means that for the time being, you lay aside your own views and values in order to enter another's world without prejudice. (1980, pp. 142–143)

This "blueprint" echoes the importance of the inner and external conditions fostering creativity and points especially to the role of the therapist in ensuring the external conditions of psychological safety and freedom. The client needs to be sure that her dream will be treated with respect. Respect in a person-centered session means the client leads the way. The client can find her own meaning if she feels safe enough to be curious (psychological safety) and the meaning can be anything (psychological freedom). The client is unique, her dreams are unique and the meaning she finds and gives to her dreams is equally unique. Due to the multidimensionality and complexity of the dreaming experience, there is no one meaning, but rather bountiful meanings only understandable through and within the internal world of the client. Especially in the beginning, the counselor is by definition "more blind" than the client because she does not and cannot share the inner dream world of the client. The counselor's explicit acknowledging of her inherent "blindness" can help to alleviate some of the client's potential initial trepidation in sharing a dream.

"Frequently checking" and *"being guided"* by the responses of the client may mean that initially what is needed is a building up of the client's trust in the creative process of dreamsensing. Allowing for an experiencing and appreciating of dreams as creative, mysterious, surprising and unique stories in their own right can be enough in and of itself. A "fitness training" of the client's "internal locus of evaluation muscle" might be called for. She might need to learn to allow and bear with a "not finding meaning" – strengthening her *"tolerance for ambiguity."* In a sense, she engages in accepting the unknown, acknowledging the richness of being at the edge of awareness and becomes more able to trust the process (the functioning of the actualizing tendency) to move forward in a "right" way. Another way to engage and exercise the client's inner "aha muscle" would be by strengthening her inner sensitivity for a "true insight," with the counselor and the client together being on the "look out" for revelations of meaning from the dream. These revelations can come with a sense of surprise, a *"eureka feeling."* They might be visible or felt through bodily signals, such as a deep sigh, a spontaneous movement, tears or laughter.

Keeping in awareness the multidimensionality and complexity of the dreaming process can also ensure psychological freedom and respect for the client's internal locus of evaluation. It is important to be open to all the many possible gifts different "types" of dreams can bring. These gifts of understanding can pertain to a variety of levels, for example, the past, present, future; a deepening of experiencing; spiritual issues; health; the therapy process. Our knowledge of dreaming and dreamsensing in a person-centered counseling setting is not yet very extensive. The best and safest bet, then, is to meet all the unique and various dreams that clients bring with a nonjudgmental openness, an unconditional positive regard, appreciating the gift in everything that arises.

The therapeutic process

Aside from the possible spontaneous and surprising signs mentioned above that can arise when a dream (or part of it) makes more sense to the client within one session, it is important to also be aware of the significance of what evolves within the whole therapeutic process. There are some changes that are particular to sensing into dreams. A client's increased trust and appreciation of dreams and her inner life are vital aspects occurring throughout the therapy process. The concrete progression of the client's dreams can also give important information about the whole therapy process. For instance a series of dreams could mirror or comment on issues being brought up inside (and outside) of therapy. In addition, repetitive dreams often change or cease completely once they are understood. On a broader level the counselor can be aware about how the issues brought up by the client's dreams and her subsequent sensing into them brought about changes in the outer life of the client, getting a sense of how useful the client finds her dream sessions. Another different source of information about the therapy process is the evolving dreams of the counselor herself (see Hill & Knox, 2010).

The counselor's process

The significance of safety and of strengthening the client's internal locus of evaluation requires that the counselor be a partner with specific attributes in addition to a person-centered way of being – Rogers' *"confident companion."* The counselor can only ensure safety if she herself trusts the dreaming and meaning-creating process. The counselor needs to believe that the client can find her own way and meaning and can lead the way. Such a knowing must be rooted in the counselor's own experience of the richness of dreamsensing and in her theoretical concept of what dreaming is and what sharing dreams can do.

The counselor's theoretical concept includes her view of her own professional role: what potential "added value" her presence can bring (as Rogers points out), and also where danger can possibly lie. The counselor's confidence, trust and experience in dreamsensing will ensure the climate that the client needs. The counselor *sensitively* and *delicately* brings the attention of the client to elements she might not be aware of or is fearful of and supports the client's meaning-creating process by pointing to possible meanings. The potential "blindness" of the client while sensing into her dreams and the concomitant potential feeling of shame require that the counselor treads carefully, with as much respect as if she would be using, for example, touch.

The possible danger lies in not respecting the client's inner locus of evaluation enough and hence limiting the space the client needs to develop her own understanding of her dreaming world. Even worse, the counselor might trespass in this inner world. This situation can happen when the counselor is "blind" to her own valuing system with regard to certain types of dreams or dream elements. If the counselor is not sufficiently aware of her own ideas, beliefs, prejudices, and concepts regarding dreams in general and her client's dreams in particular, she might intervene in ways that block or even stop the therapeutic process. She might for instance move ahead of the client, going too fast, prematurely offering an idea about the meaning of the dream or about the dreamsensing process, thereby creating irritation and resistance in the client. Thus the counselor has to be acutely attuned to any signals coming from the client signaling a blockage in the process due to an overly active input on the part of the counselor (another instance of Rogers' *"frequently checking"*).

One way of approaching this danger zone is to be aware of times when a "certainty" arises within the counselor – a sign that the counselor has found the "true" meaning for the client. When the counselor is able to view this "certainty" as a danger signal, as a sign that she is close to imposing her own views on the client, the counselor can then consciously let go and move back to the territory of the unknown, until the dreamer has found her own way.

Lastly, dreamsensing will enliven both the client and the counselor. It will not only help the counselor to come two steps closer to the client's perspective (see Chapter 1) but will also aid the counselor in strengthening her person-centered way of being with the client. The ongoing experiencing of the uniqueness of the client coupled with the constant necessity of letting go of all preconceptions naturally results in this enlivening. The habitual *"laying aside of views and values"* is, thus, a form of client-centered discipline. Through dreamsensing the counselor stays closer to the mysterious, the unknown, the edge of awareness and is thereby living counseling as an art form.

Summary of the main points

- Dreamsensing within therapy can be viewed as a creative process. Client and therapist thus need to foster in themselves Rogers' three inner conditions: openness to experience; an internal locus of evaluation; an ability to play with elements and concepts. It is the role of the therapist to also ensure

Rogers' two outer conditions: psychological safety and freedom.

- More so than with other issues brought into therapy sessions, dreams can make the client feel especially vulnerable and in a way "blind." This partial blindness requires of the client a strong inner compass, or an easily accessible internal locus of evaluation.

- Due to the special vulnerability and "blindness" connected with dream-sharing, the client's propensity to feel shame is a pivotal issue.

- Particularly at the start of a therapy process it seems imperative for the counselor to assess where the client situates herself with regard to her dreaming experiencing. The client might need an initial input by the therapist as to why dreamsensing is valuable and what it might entail.

- The therapist can use Rogers' description of an "empathic way of being" as a basic "blueprint" for how to accompany a client with her dream.

- The counselor's confidence, trust and experience in dreamsensing will help ensure the climate the client needs.

- The counselor must have a high sensitivity for potential danger zones in dreamsensing due to the "blindness" and shame propensities of the client. These can be encountered when the counselor limits the space the client needs for her exploration. Also trespassing in the inner world of the client might occur due to the "blindness" of the counselor. An extra safety measure can be the counselor's habitual checking within herself for the potential danger signal of a premature "certainty" in the meaning of the dream.

- Especially with regard to dreamsensing, there is a constant necessity on the part of the counselor to lay aside her preconceptions and value judgments. This is a special form of discipline, enhancing the client-centeredness of the counselor.

3

Experiencing the Territory
with Three Dreams

After charting the territory of dreamsensing on a theoretical and practical level I want to turn now to the more concrete and personal level. In this chapter, I want to give you a first-hand impression of what a person-centered dream session might entail and how much they can differ. In preparation for writing this book I had dream sessions with three women, each representing a different path of dreamsensing within the person-centered world (see also Chapter 1). The first dream session with Helga Lemke stands for what I have termed the "relational" person-centered approach. The second dream session with Barbara McGavin (who would not call herself a therapist, rather a Focusing guide) gives an impression of how Focusing and dreamsensing can blend. The third dream session with Clara Hill is the most elaborate, filling three hours (compared with the 50-minute sessions of the other two). Hill's approach I termed "structural dreamsensing" due to the fact that it has three stages: (a) exploration, (b) insight, and (c) action.

Chapters 3 and 4 actually go hand in hand. In this chapter I will concentrate on the perspective of the client, starting with the client's dream narrative, followed by the dream session and ending with a summary from the client's perspective. In Chapter 4 the perspective of the therapist/guide will be the focal point, explaining what each was doing by illuminating some of the theoretical underpinnings of the three pathways. Some readers might prefer to have more information on the theory behind the three approaches before reading the dream sessions to understand what each therapist/guide is doing and how they differ. They might want to read Chapter 4 before this one. Personally, I find it harder to delve into a dream session and follow both perspectives of client and therapist at the same time. I realize that reading the transcript of a dream session is very different from reading the rest of this book. (I am a very avid reader and have in the past often skipped over exactly these "other" parts, therapy session transcripts as well as the exercises that are sometimes included. I have experienced over the years though, that it is precisely these "other" parts that can be the most interesting.)

The following dream sessions are not part of a counseling process. They stand by themselves. Clara Hill has called her model of a dream session a "mini-therapy." Within an ongoing therapy process a session like one of the following would come within a therapeutic context, i.e., there would be sessions following this one (or preceding it). Future sessions would pick up on the insights and experiences generated in these dream sessions. One could view the three dream sessions as examples of what an initial session might be like with a client who is very eager to understand her dreaming world and happening either within or outside of a formal therapy setting.

In Chapter 2 I brought up the question of how the client moves within her dreamsensing landscape. Situating myself along an imagined continuum, I would place myself more at one end with extensive experience in dreamsensing and generally valuing my dreams highly. I am an experienced Focuser and in that regard consider my "internal locus of evaluation muscle" well "trained." Practicing Focusing has sharpened my sense of what will take me deeper in a process and also of what might take me out. Through ample dream sharing and Focusing I am used to sharing something while it newly emerges, not knowing how it will emerge or what will come. My "blindness" regarding the meaning of the three dreams was profound initially, however, I certainly knew a lot about what the process of dreamsensing would be like. So, all in all I would describe myself as an example of a client who is more "far-sighted" than "blind."

Due to my prior experiences and knowledge about the process, the safety issue I elaborated on in Chapter 2 was in some ways not such a critical issue in my sessions. Even though I had never had a dream session (or any other sort of counseling session) with any of the three therapists, I had a strong sense of trust in their way of working. Being trained in person-centered (or Focusing) ways I expected them to follow Rogers' "blueprint" of empathically being with me (see Chapter 2).

- With Helga Lemke I had in fact only had one face-to-face conversation about dreams and person-centered ways of working with them and this was a couple of years prior to the dream session. The following face-to-face dream session with Helga Lemke was originally in German.
- Barbara McGavin I had met as a Focusing workshop leader of a week-long "Treasure Maps to the Soul" also a couple of years prior to this dream session on the phone.
- My first conversation with Clara Hill was the dream session itself, also on the phone.

The sessions are for the most part transcribed in full – I have put […] wherever I have omitted a couple of sentences.

I chose a different dream to work with for each session, because, as the saying goes, "you cannot step into the same river twice." The initial experience of "not knowing" at the beginning of the dream-sharing would be lost if the same dream were the subject of different sessions. A dream session brings the dream memory "back to life" adding depth and bringing new meaning to the dream; the dream memory can also change because of this. Experiencing a different level of meaning is what makes dreamsensing so special. It contains the thrill of discovery and surprise, similar to solving a puzzle. The pioneering exploration is different from those that follow. This of course does in no way mean that subsequent expeditions can't be as helpful, meaningful or useful. It is just easier to discern what has come as a new revelation, when we start out with virtually knowing nothing. This was the case with the three dreams I chose to work with. I couldn't fathom what they were about apart from the dream story I remembered.

The "museum dream": Relational person-centered dreamsensing with Helga Lemke

The museum dream

I am in a big museum. In the beginning there is a scene with a museum employee and a disabled woman. The disabled woman comes into the museum and talks to the employee in an intimate way. The employee greets the woman very warmly and asks her where she has been so long. They talk for a while and I listen in. After a while I want to move on. The employee clears the path for me and thanks me for automatically giving the disabled woman a program of the exhibition. The disabled woman is sitting in a wheelchair and I had bent down in order to talk with her. She then gets up. In order to stand up she had to get rid of a lot of plastic clamps.

I go into the museum. Then a teacher comes with his school class. The museum employee has to tell him that the exhibition has already closed, that there is nothing to see at the moment. The teacher is very annoyed about this and can't understand it all.

I go further through a hallway with wooden pine walls until I reach the very big entrance hall of the museum. I deliberate whether I should call a friend in California, or walk down the stairs to the bathroom (but I only have socks on). Then at that moment my mother taps me on the shoulder from behind and tells me to look forward and not backward. I ask her how she came here. She says, she and my father had spontaneously decided to come and meet me here. I say that it's great that we met so easily in this big room with all the people. (Dreamt on March 1, 2011 and shared with Helga Lemke (H) face to face on March 11, 2011.)

The dream session

H: So you wake up, your mother turns up, you are unsure what you should do.

A: I especially remember feeling, what a nice surprise, how nice that she found me so easily in this big room with all those people.

H: Museum, what comes to your mind when you think of museum?

A: Hmm ... not much really. I thought I would choose this dream, because I really don't know what it's about. So museum, what comes up is that I like some museums better than others. The typical old-fashioned ones make me really tired. But ones like the one in the dream, with modern art are nicer. Even there though, I get tired after a while.

[... deleted short part on recollections of former museum visits in waking life]

H: In the dream, were you in the museum to look at something, or were you there by chance?

A: In the dream, I am there. I observe a lot. I observe how the disabled woman talks with the museum employee, and how the employee deals with the teacher. Especially at the beginning I observe a lot. I don't have any feeling about what I actually wanted to do there, it's not there.

H: It's not there, it's more the museum employee, someone that supervises ... and a disabled person ...

A: The employee is in the entrance area like a ticket seller. She is the one who is in charge, she is the one who deals with the teacher. The intimacy of her relationship with the disabled visitor surprises me.

H: Yes, you mentioned that, they seemed so intimate, they knew each other.

A: Yes, that really surprised me. You come to a museum once a year, it's not like your corner shop, where you build up a customer relationship. Here it was different. Here there is not only me observing, but also I am being observed. The employee thanks me for building up this connection with the disabled woman. Also, there is that moment where I try to connect with her in a good way, I bend down to be on eye-level with her. But here the museum is more like the backdrop.

H: Yes, the dream seems to be for you more about these three persons: the teacher, the museum supervisor, and the disabled person. And here the question comes up, in which way are they like parts of you? A competent woman, a disabled woman, and a teacher.

A: Yes. (pause) I've often dreamt of a disabled person and I have sometimes thought that that could be a part of me, a disabled aspect of me.

H: Is there something in you that can't grow, can't be upright?

A: Yeah, hmm … I have to take some time to sense in me how that would be as a team …

H: … or first one person at a time …

A: Hmm. (pause) Yes, the museum employee would be a familiar part, one who is in charge, rules, regulation, manages …

H: … feeling competent …

A: Yeah.

H: … being in charge, feeling responsible …

A: Yeah.

H: So this part you feel inside …

A: Yes, and also the part that talks with the annoyed teacher. That part is also easy …

H: So, that you feel inside …

A: Yeah. (pause) This disabled woman, who talks so much at the beginning …

H: … that is intimate with the other part …

A: Hmm. (pause)

H: … with whom you also connect …

A: Hmm. (pause) There are many areas where I feel I am disabled, or holding back.

H: … can't go like I want to go …

A: Yes, lay down all the clamps or braces … This is really interesting, with this supervisor, the intimacy, it's mostly about giving up control.

H: So, you know about this part but you also control it strongly.

A: Hmm. (pause) Trusting that I can stand on my own feet. The plastic clamps give a sort of support. Then there is a rationalizing, or control part that gives it support but also disables it, because it is more a part that can also be without those clamps.

H: That wants to grow, but also can't grow with the clamps on.

A: Hmm. (pause)

H: It's controlled too much?

A: (sigh) Yes, it's a process. The image is nice, the intimate conversation between the two, they know each other. So I ask myself, why does she always come to the museum? Also a wondering about why doesn't she just put down those braces and walk if she can? But also interesting, the dynamic in the dream. That the "dream-I" gives her a program …

H: … that you are watching …

A: Yes, watching but also actively giving her the program. There is almost more contact with the disabled woman, with that part, than with the museum employee – there it is more of an observing of her.

H: That you should pay more attention to this part?

A: Yes. That's what makes it so interesting that the supervising part thinks that it is good.

H: That you pay more attention to it.

A: Yes.

H: … So that the more rational part also finds it a good idea that you pay attention to the disabled part.

A: Hmm.

H: … towards the part that wants to grow within you.

A: Yes. To take up the same vantage point …

H: To sink down into your knees and look …

A: Yes. It's a special form of paying attention, of being aware. It fits with this person or this part.

H: Yes. So the dream is telling you, look at that, accept that, be good to it.

A: (pause) I give her the program and get praised for that. Hmm. The teacher also comes because of the program, the exhibition is over.

H: Yes, the teacher, what does he tell you?

A: (laugh) Well, indignation, a part that gets really mad, I know that part well. However, in a situation like that I find it hard to imagine. I would know that the exhibition is over. I'm not the type that wouldn't know that. That is why here, there is something like, hmm … this is not typical. If I would come and the exhibition would be over, I would be mad about myself but I wouldn't be annoyed that the exhibition is now closed …

H: You would be annoyed?

A: No, I would be mad at myself, but not turn it outward …

H: Well, the teacher has a certain symbolic significance.

A: Yes. He is responsible for the whole class.

H: Ah, yes the class is with him …

A: He brought all the pupils along with him. He really is in a bad situation. He brought along a lot of people and now there is nothing, nothing happens. (sigh) He's not acting responsibly, he's falling short in his duties.

H: Is there something in you that wants something that's not possible?

A: There is always a lot (laugh) ... but now, with all those children ... something in me that ...

H: Well he is also a person of respect, a teacher ...

A: Yes. That is what stays ambivalent, or stays puzzling. Something like this doesn't happen to a teacher. I can't imagine something like this happening.

H: It should not have happened to him ...

A: Yes, that shouldn't have happened to him, not with the whole class and everything. That part I know, that I have certain expectations of myself, of a certain quality, or of perfectionism. Something like this can't really happen to me.

H: Aha, what does the dream have to say about this?

A: Hmm ... In the dream there is the situation between the employee, the supervisor and the disabled person and the teacher. The employee says, it's not possible, it's clear the exhibition is over. But the part, if there is a part that orchestrates a situation like that. For example, when I come too late to an important meeting ... hmm. Here we come again to the part, the teacher part that turns his annoyance outwards, he says the supervisor is wrong. Hmm. That would be when I for example come too late, the part that caused the lateness would be annoyed with my controlling part, instead of looking at what caused it by itself.

H: Yes.

A: Hmm. That resonates ... I can see a connection here. When something like that happens, always the supervising part – the controlling part that checks and manages everything – feels like it was inadequate, wasn't watching out enough. So I should go a step further, was there something, a part that … it was not due to the lack of control, it was due to the part …

H: That wasn't planned right.

A: Yes. That didn't want to plan it, or had its reasons for not looking to see if the exhibition was over.

H: … made it incomplete somewhere …

A: Yes.

H: And yes, you said you are a perfectionist, so it's hard to give that part more room.

A: Yes. Usually it is a reason (laugh) to turn the screws tighter. The controlling part has to function better, you know …

H: Yes, yes.

A: When something like that happens, oh, then the control is not strong enough. Instead, I have to see that the problem isn't caused by the screws. I have to look at the other part, it has its own dynamic.

H: Yes. So the dream is saying have a look at that.

A: That was also the beginning, where I said, I can't understand the teacher at all. When I looked at the teacher, it was like in waking life, I have no empathy with him. Hmm. So there are two parts that need attention, independent of the supervisor.

H: Yes, that want to live their own lives and need to be looked at: "look, I am also here."

A: Hmm.

H: That don't always want to be besieged from above.

A: Yes. (pause) Yes, that makes sense.

H: So this part of the dream is clear so far? And now the dream goes further. You are walking out and you meet your mother.

A: Yes. I am walking through a long hallway with wooden paneling and then I arrive in a huge entrance hall of the museum. There is a moment where I don't know what I should do. I don't feel like I'm dressed right ... going to the toilet and not having any shoes on.

H: So there is some insecurity ...

A: Yes, some insecurity, it doesn't really fit well ...

H: ... who am I really?

A: Yes, who am I, what do I want to do, do I want to call or what ...?

H: It fits well with the first part of the dream, right?

A: Yes.

H: It generates insecurity if I have to suddenly look at these two dream figures.

A: Yes.

H: And in this sense of insecurity you meet your mother ...

A: Yes, from the back. There's a tap, tap tap. We are here. (pause) Very spontaneously, very surprising, just like a gift.

H: So that your mother is a gift in this situation.

A: That we meet so easily, that she is there so fast. There's a connection with the "what shall I do? "where shall I go?" from before. And then it's so easy, so unexpectedly easy. (pause)

H: What might your mother stand for?

A: ... caring, attentive, mindful, supportive. (pause) My mother called me yesterday morning for example and surprised me. She knew that I was not well informed on what was happening in the world at the moment and wanted to tell me that the trains were on strike, that I might not be able to come to meet you in Hanover. I was surprised that she thought about my plans to travel to you and that it's a part of my book project and important. That is a concrete example, similar to in the dream, where I am surprised that she is suddenly there.

H: So this part says, you don't have to be so insecure, the part that is caring and suddenly is there?

A: Yes, I think this question of the easiness – that it is not so hard to connect with this part. But it still has something surprising.

H: So the surprising part is still not clear?

A: Well, I am trying to imagine this part in me, who is there, who is attentive …

H: … a part you can depend on …

A: Yes, a part I can depend on, but where the connection is so easy – and this still has something surprising.

H: So, it's really not so hard to look at the other parts, could that be the connection?

A: Yes, because this connection to the mother part is there and also easy to come upon. I think the trust in this easiness still has to grow.

H: Yes, it surprises you that it is there. That you are not alone, that you do not have to keep this insecurity.

A: Yes, it is really very surprising.

H: So, the resources are in you.

A: Yes. (pause) My mother also tells me in the dream to look forward and not backwards. I understand that as a signal to go forward more and not to preoccupy myself with what has been.

H: Yes, it's probably also connected with having found a new apartment, but the old is still burdensome for you.

A: Yes. (pause)

H: Look ahead and don't look back, she says.

A: Yes. And she comes so surprisingly from behind and taps me …

H: That's a look, watch out, be aware of what you have in you …

A: Yes.

H: How are you feeling now?

A: Good. It's always wonderful – theoretically I know this – but when in practice it's wonderful when the dream opens up and you see things from a totally different perspective.

H: When you came you said you had no idea what it meant and now it's resolved.

A: Yes. Yes. Very nice.

The client's summary

After exploring the first part of the dream in some detail we come to the conclusion that the dream might be more about the characters than the setting of the museum. Prompted by Helga Lemke, I start sensing into the three persons, the museum employee, the disabled woman and the teacher as if they were parts of myself. I start by wondering about the relationship between the disabled woman and the employee, why they are so familiar with each other, after all, the museum is not a corner shop. I wonder about how the disabled woman can stand on her two feet once she gives up the support of those plastic parts. I come to an understanding of how in waking life, there is a part of me that has everything under control (museum employee) and how surprisingly it is in a constant warm dialogue with a handicapped part of me that is trying to stand on its own feet. Also the supervising part thanked me for communicating so easily with the disabled part of me. So the dreaming self is connecting with something that is growing and my supervising part is also taking care, checking in on this disabled part. I link this to situations in my waking life, where something wants to grow, and is being "kept" in check (braces on). The dream and the dream session lead me to sense deeper into the parts in me that want to grow, that need more of my "full" attention.

Then there is also a part (teacher) that finds the source of trouble lies outside of himself. I wonder about how the teacher can be so annoyed with the museum, when in fact it is his own fault and his inability to plan, which put him in this situation.

The connected valuing question within myself, "How can he be so annoyed?" shows an inner conflict that also arises in my waking life. When I make a mistake in my planning in waking life, there is no empathy with the part of me that caused the mistake. This lack of self-empathy causes me to be harsh and judgmental with myself and closes off a possible understanding of the deeper cause that led to the mistake. Up to now I would have sought the source of trouble in not having things sufficiently under control (the supervising part's fault). Learning from the dream, in the future I will want to look deeper and sense if there might not be another reason, a part that up to now I haven't even considered looking at (seen from my initial waking logic a teacher finding himself in that situation is by definition impossible).

Coming to the last part of the dream I sense into my feelings when my mother tapped me on the shoulder. What came was the sense of support and also the surprise in how easy it was to meet up. A connection with the internal resources that I carry within me, that nurture and support me. Sensing into this part of the dream gave me a clearer impression of that support and an idea that it is easier for me to connect with it than I had thought.

So, after the dream session, what would be an initial answer to the question: What was the dream trying to tell me? The dream sketched my current waking life situation and inner conflicts, my insecurity about how to move forward (at the top of the stairs) and showed me that I can have easy access to the inner resources I need. Most certainly there are still many more relevant meanings to be found in the dream (and I have found many since!), however given the limits of a 50-minute session, I had the feeling I had harvested a substantial amount of what the dream had to offer.

The "damp and crowded cloakroom dream": Focusing and dreamsensing with Barbara McGavin

For readers unfamiliar with Focusing here is a short note on what a Focusing process entails: The client senses into the body, staying at the edge of awareness – with a "felt sense"; letting new words, or images come that describe the felt sense; eventually leading to a bodily felt new understanding – "felt shift." During this bodily sensing for the "right" symbols or words it is very helpful for someone to reflect back the exact wording of what one has created, letting the client feel the bodily resonance of the newly found words, checking within for their "rightness." This bodily checking within is a slow process and can take up to a few minutes. See also Appendix A.

The damp and crowded cloakroom dream

I am walking down some steps. I don't know where I am going, but other people are also walking down. At the end there is a cloakroom, a wardrobe, a place to hang up coats. It is all very full and the floor is wet. I only have socks on. I try out a door – it leads into the building and I see there is another place to hang up coats. It is all dry and empty and I walk there and I see there is a glass door and windows. And behind that there is a really big room and at the very end of that there is a friend of mine sitting, talking on the phone. She waves at me and signals that she doesn't have any time to talk to me now. There is a woman who works there and I notice you can only get tea from a machine and by the cup, and the woman who works there offers me a tea by the name of "mountain something or other" and there were also other sorts of teas, like "mint medley." The woman tells me about a big event that has taken place and now she has to do all the financial calculations for it. (Dreamt on June 27, 2011 shared with Barbara McGavin (B) on the phone on July 11, 2011.)

The dream session

A: So that was the dream. The feeling of the first part going down those stairs, in that small, cramped space with the wet floor, has a different feel to the other building, with its glass and the wood – it's more open and spacious and dry.

B: Yes, you are really sensing the difference between these two parts of the dream. One that is like small, cramped, wet, the other is open, spacious, dry with glass and wood. Both of those are there. And it feels like they are really two different parts with two different qualities to them.

A: Hmm.

B: Yeah. Maybe just getting a sense of the quality of each of those parts, maybe there is more that wants to be known about that.

A: Well the first part, there is a sadness somewhere to it. Maybe also a heaviness.

B: Yeah. You're sensing maybe there is a kind of sad or heavy quality to that first part.

A: Hmm.

B: Yeah.

A: And walking down those steps, not really knowing where I am going, with all those other people and that dark, damp, full. There are no windows there, sort of like a cellar place.

B: Yeah. So this place has no windows, it's dark, kind of like a cellar. And as you in the dream walk down these steps you don't know where you are going.

A: Hmm.

B: And there are people going there, like there are a lot of people that are going in this direction.

A: (pause) The other, the second part, seems so much in contrast with that. It seems so open, so spacious, there's my friend sitting there, and there is this woman working there who is nice. There are a lot less people, just these two.

B: So in this big space, there are only these two people and one of them is your friend who doesn't have time to talk with you right now, but acknowledges you, waves to you. And this other person who is working there, she has a nice feel to her, like a pleasantness.

A: (pause) And when I walk down to the first part without shoes. It is wet on the ground and I just have socks on. And I lose that, maybe because it is dry, but it's not an issue in the second part.

B: Something there about not having shoes and the ground is wet, the floor is wet in the first one. So there is a quality in there, something about that as well.

A: (pause) And that's where the sadness is, not having the shoes in that wet place.

B: Something about not having the shoes that brings sad, something feels sad there.

A: Hmm…and an urge to get out of there.

B: Something just wants to get out of there, in the dream wants to get out of that space. … So here we have a place where you in the dream and the dream are kind of disagreeing.

A: Hmm.

B: Like the dream brings you all of this, gives you this space, brings you down all these stairs to this place. So, maybe we can make a space for whatever it is that created this space and brought you down the stairs.

A: (pause) That seems like a good… (laugh) a lot comes up with that. There is a whole wave of warmth in my body, resonating, a sense of, yes this is important. And there is another, there is a part that is saying (laugh) but it's really cold and wet there, a part that's pleading for the logic of fleeing.

B: So there's something important here. And there's something saying, but it's cold and wet here, I don't want to be there, it wants to flee. Freely acknowledging it, of course it doesn't want you to stay, it doesn't want to stay in a place that is cold and wet.

Maybe there is something more it doesn't want staying in that cold and wet place.

A: It's also all those people and the crowdedness.

B: Something about all those people and the crowdedness …

A: No room.

B: Yeah, there is no room.

A: (pause) When I go back to the idea that there is a reason for the dream for bringing me there, there is still all that warmth.

B: When you sense there is some good reason the dream brought you there, there is this feeling of warmth in your body.

A: (pause) And the belly it's sort of a mixture of excitement and anxiousness.

B: Something is excited and anxious there in your belly.

A: (pause) Whereas the part that is saying: it is so cold and damp and crowded, feels more like a … heady thinking part.

B: Yeah, you're noticing the part that's saying it feels cold and crowded, it feels more like a thought, … in your body, something like that.

A: (pause) Now it almost feels I am trapped with both of that. Like they are holding each other in … how would you say, stagnation …

B: So there's a kind of stagnant quality, a stagnation, feeling that comes, like there is a trap, or holding each other somehow.

A: (pause) Almost like the part – that being there, that resonance, that warmth in my body and that excitement in my belly – it's almost if that is saying stay. And the other part that feels it's so damp and cold and crowded is on my head, partly by the eyes and it is saying go.

B: So you are sensing there in your body where it feels warm and excited it's saying stay. And the other you feel in your eyes and head it is saying go. You might notice who they are saying it to.

A: (pause) Well, spontaneously I would say me. But then there is a sense that it is a good question. And then there is a sense of not being able to grasp it.

B: Well it might not lead anywhere. But there is certainly a sense of one side, like it's saying stay, it's wanting something, somebody to stay and the other is saying go, like it's wanting something or somebody to go. And it might be you, it might be your awareness. But, at least we know that. (pause) There may be something that each side wants or doesn't want for …

A: … and now I couldn't hear you …

B: Maybe sensing or inviting each to say more about what it wants or doesn't want if you stay or go.

A: Well the stay is, it's as if it's saying if you stay in that crowded, damp, place just to sense what would have happened if I would have stayed there and not moved to the building. And the go part is the one saying go to that building.

B: So stay is like seeing what would have happened if you'd stayed. Like it wants some further opening or unfolding happening. The other is just like, I want you to go to the building, where the light is, openness is, where the spaciousness is.

A: (pause) And it's almost as if the feeling in my body mirrors the dream feeling. Like it's the opposite. The stay is this warm energetic feeling in the body. And in the dream it was in a place that's not that way at all. And the part that says go has more of a pulling down, or more of a holding quality, a tight quality.

B: So you are noticing how the feeling in your body is almost a mirror image of what it was like in your dream. So in your body it is warm whereas it says stay with this place of cold in the dream. Whereas the place that says go has sort of this pulling down tight kind of quality.

A: I think that's what's making the, what's generating the tangle, that trapped feeling, or that feeling that they are hindering each other, or keeping each other in place.

B: It feels like that is what is keeping them in place. A kind of something feeling trapped in there.

A: (deep sigh) It's as if the part of me that wants to understand it is getting in there, saying this isn't logical, this is the other way around. Trying to sort it out and not getting anywhere.

B: Yeah. That's very paradoxically logical, that it's like this, that it feels like backwards or …

A: Hmm.

B: Just really acknowledging this is how it is right now.

A: Hmm. (deep breath, long pause with deep sighs intermittently) … It's an instance of experiencing how hard (sigh), how hard it can be to accept a bodily response that is so clear yet turns what I thought on its head.

B: You're really recognizing this is an instance of how hard it can be for something in you to accept that bodily sense that turns something on its head, what seems to be, when you sense it in your body, your body says no this is how I am responding to it, or this is what the response is here.

A: (pause) It's like when, I don't know, when I dream of something. I wake up with a feeling that is anxious, or feeling that's not nice, that I'm happy that I'm awake, that it was a dream. And it takes all my conscious effort to remember it and stay with it and write it down, to work with it afterwards knowing that it's something important and it will bring me further. And so this feels like it, in a way, there is this clear bodily sense that there is some reason that I am in that place, that dark, full, damp, wardrobe, cloakroom or whatever. And then there's that part that's thinking that can't be. That just can't be.

B: You're really sensing the part that's really going like yes, there's something really important about being down here in this damp, dark, cool. And then this other part that is in effect going it can't be, like it just wants to flee, wants to get away from all of that.

You're also really noticing how it happens, like waking up from a dream and being glad to be out of it and how hard it is to turn back towards it sometimes. And in your body there is this real kind of warm, excited, curious, little bit kind of anxious.

A: (pause) So I am wondering what would be a good way to get more of a sense of this?

B: Well, there are a number of things. Maybe just taking a little time to sense what needs your attention here in this whole thing, there is a lot going on. It might be the part that wants to pull away or turn away from what feels uncomfortable. It might be getting a sense of that whole uncomfortable place, that something feels is uncomfortable. Maybe even saying hello to it. Like saying: hello, you there, hello, this place here.

A: So sort of like getting more of a sense of the part that looked for a door and opened the door to the building?

B: You could do that. One part to go with.

A: (pause) There is a ... I was wondering whether in the dream this room might have felt like it feels now, more like in that warm belly sort of feeling. And if there is something that made me view it differently. There is almost like a feeling of, the warmth is like a grounded feeling in the body and this pull away like it is in the head, almost a sense of, as if that might have been in the dream, as if something, pulled me out of there. Like the head pulled me out or something pulled me out. I have a warmth on my right, no my left outer hand, an area of warmth on the skin and on my right arm on the side, forearm. I don't know what that is connected to.

B: So you are noticing this warmth in your hand, your left outer hand, your right arm and there's this feeling of how, there's this warmth connected also to the room that spacious room and you're sensing that in your body ...

A: No, to the cloakroom ...

B: Oh, to the cloakroom ...

A: Yes to the wet place, that is what is so weird about it. This warm feeling in the body …

B: Is connected with the colder place in the dream, the cloakroom place.

A: Right, right. And then there is sort of a pull if I sense into the place of looking for the door, it sort of feels like that pull in the head, it's like pulling me out of there.

B: Like something in your head pulling you out of there, but your body feeling is warm. We have about four minutes.

A: (pause) How much time do we still have?

B: A couple of minutes.

A: OK. It feels like the warmth is moving up, it is now below my shoulders. It is as if a boundary is moving up through the body.

B: Your sensing that warmth moving up through your body. It is up to your shoulders now. (pause) And maybe letting whatever still needs attention know you are willing to come back if it needs it.

A: Hmm … Now. That's a good place to come to an end.

B: OK.

The client's summary

It is clear from the beginning that the two parts of the dream have a different feel to them. Through sensing into the dream in a Focusing way, the depth of the experience of how it feels to be in the damp and cramped wardrobe place of the dream is literally "fleshed out." This fleshing out is a slow process, the pauses sometimes filling up two to three minutes of sensing into the body, letting the vague evolve and become clearer. Through this process, I develop a clear bodily sense, a felt sense of being in that place. There comes a discordance: bodily it feels good to be in that place and simultaneously there is a cognitive wondering about how that can be, given the dampness, the crowdedness of the place. A bodily awareness arises that there is something "right" or important about being in that dream space, and at the same time there is another pull within me to move on to open the door and move to that lighter and dryer room. For quite some time I just sense into this bodily felt paradox, I stay with the clear bodily felt sense of the damp cold place and with the wonder "how can it be good there?" I am deepening and exploring my experience of this paradox. It is also an experiencing of patiently and curiously staying with the unknown and experiencing how hard it sometimes is to stay and not move away. At the end of the session I realize the parallel to sensing into difficult dreams, how the bodily felt sense of the dream is so strong and at the same time there is an intellectual pull away from it, to forget it and get on with waking life.

The "nothing is set up dream":
Structural dreamsensing with Clara Hill

The nothing is set up dream

I arrive at a place where we are going to hold a seminar – where we are going to select our volunteers that have all applied. And some of the candidates, the participants, are already there. But the rooms haven't been set up yet. The chairs are not all set up and in one room the participants have put their bikes. Now I tell them to take the bikes out. All of the sudden an image of a guy, of a man appears on the floor, on the ground, like a visual image like you would see on TV or on "skype," just the face. And he is talking to me, he's somehow connected to the Belgian diplomacy, and he says he wants to talk to a participant or he wants us to send a participant out, a woman. Next to me is a colleague of mine, who is also a lawyer, and I ask him – because I don't understand all of what this guy is asking me – and I ask him what this is about. My colleague gets annoyed that I don't understand it and get it. I get annoyed at him for being so openly in conflict with me in front of the participants. But he says that we are not required by law to send this woman out to these people. We can just ignore the request. I continue to set up chairs. There are different rooms, they are sort of connected. I am trying to find the best place to talk with all the participants. The chairs are all different. Some are really big chairs, like living room sort of chairs. They are standing in the middle of the room, and I would like to have them all along the wall. So I ask the participants to help me. Then I notice there are not enough chairs. There is a little room connected, a storage room or something. I take chairs out of there. But there are still not enough. There are smaller chairs, and I get them. They set up a microphone system in the front, in a place where I didn't want to speak. I wanted to speak somewhere in the middle where the three rooms are connected, so most people could see me. Then I am wondering whether I should not use a microphone and just talk like I always do. Or whether I should ask all the participants to come forward and stand while we are introducing the program. (Dreamt on July 18, 2011 shared with Clara Hill (C) on the phone the same day.)

The dream session

The exploration stage

A: And that's where I woke up.

C: How did you feel when you woke up?

A: It was a bit of a … it still had that feeling of the dream where it's frustrating because things aren't set up like they are supposed to and there is not that much time and it's not working out as I would want it to.

C: Kind of frustrated, annoyed, kind of feeling out of control.

A: Yeah. After, the next thought of course was whether this would be a dream to bring up today. And then I thought, well it seems to me to be a pretty normal, everyday sort of dream and I was a bit disappointed. And then I thought, well, this might be perfect, because it's a normal sort of dream and not extraordinary.

C: Sort of, kind of feeling like maybe it is not good enough or maybe it is better because it is not a big dream, major …

A: Right.

C: Kind of a lot of feelings going on.

A: Hmm.

C: Then you said as you got closer to the end you got more nervous about talking to me, nervous about the dream about all this, how's it all going to go.

A: Yeah. Exactly. Will it be good for the book or not. Will I, how can I manage my different roles, my being the dreamer talking to you and me, being the writer.

C: OK. So wondering if you can just be present and just experience it, versus thinking about all the things you have to do around it.

A: Yeah. Exactly.

C: How are you feeling right now?

A: I'm feeling good. It's still a mixture of excitement and a lot of curiosity. Mostly curious and excited.

C: A little bit more relaxed.

A: Yeah.

C: So if you could go through the dream and pick out like three to five major images that really are key that you would want to work on.

A: OK. So I would definitely choose the guy who's talking, the film sort of way on the ground, because that seems like a science fiction sort of dream aspect. That really falls out of the dream.

C: OK. That's the Belgian guy with …

A: Right, exactly. And then I'd also choose the sense of the chairs not being in the right place. And maybe because I have no idea, it sort of seems, the bicycles that are in the room. The bicycles of the participants. Let's see. Maybe I would also choose this set-up of the rooms, 'cause they are sort of … 'cause it's not one room, one big room. They are connected but it's not really a setting you would have for a seminar like that. So now I have four, and you said three to five?

C: How about this lawyer colleague?

A: OK. We can do him too.

C: So. Let's try to get back into it and kind of go sequentially …

A: OK.

C: So the bikes seem like the first major image. Can you describe that a little more thoroughly for me, you know just picture yourself being right there and trying to put me in the …

A: Yeah, it was a room and they had put their bikes, the whole floor was filled with bikes. They just, you know, put them down on the floor. So the bikes were flat on the floor and they were filling up the whole floor. There was no room for anything else. And there was a sense that the participants had brought them inside, because they were scared there would be thieves, if they would put them outside they would get stolen. But it was definitely not a place – you know it was a place where we were going to meet and put up chairs – so definitely not a place for bikes. So I had to tell them to take all the bikes out.

C: So is this the same room that you described or tell me a bit more about the room.

A: There were different rooms and they were connected. And this was the room that was, I would say the farthest away from the mike but it was the closest, where the people would enter. And it wasn't a big room and there was nothing else in it. I mean it all had a sense of, like a bungalow, just it was the ground floor sort of setting. There were windows. But it was more like a boxlike sort of thing. It was more like a straightforward sort of building, like maybe a modern or cheap sort of building. So it wasn't like an old building and it looked more like it was, it had more a sense of like a bungalow, something that was, didn't have the feeling like it was, you know, very – how do I say – a structure that will stay for the next 200 years.

C: So, not terribly well constructed, more, not solid.

A: Right.

C: And these participants, what are they like, can you tell me about them, the people who have the bikes?

A: Right. So in my work we send out long-term volunteers to different countries to do voluntary service. And those are usually young adults. Usually, they do that after school. That's why they were there, they were participants, who applied for a program and this was the start of a three-day seminar, where we would, you know, get into discussion groups or interviews and decide who will go to which project, to which country. So they are young, they are at the end of their teens or beginning of their twenties. And they are mostly very motivated and eh …

C: Idealistic kind of …

A: Idealistic and engaged. Yeah. And especially of course here at this moment, they want something from our organization and we want of course something from them but they are applying for a place in our program so they usually also do what you want them to do. So if I would ask them to take their bikes out they would do it right away.

C: So, they are eager to please?

A: Right, eager to please.

C: So, are there, do you see a lot of these applicants and you are just selecting a few for a few spots?

A: There are more applicants than spots, places. So we can't take them all, but I would say like, maybe 80% we can take. But in the dream it was at the beginning so it hadn't started yet. It was before it would start. But the participants, some of them were already there. So it wasn't … they weren't all there, but some of them who would come earlier, were already there.

C: And these bikes, can you describe them more?

A: They seem to, well they look like new bikes. They are like street bikes, they are not racing bikes. But they did look like they weren't very cheap, so there is something about that I can understand that they were afraid that they might get stolen. So there was a sense of understanding why they brought them inside. I didn't understand why they all laid them on the floor like that, flat. But I understood why they thought it would be better and safer to put them inside.

C: So you understand but you're kind of annoyed too? It sounds like they are lying flat on the floor, they are taking up a lot of space …

A: Yeah, but it's more like oh it's something I have to deal with. But I'm not annoyed at them for doing it. It's more like I have to deal with this also.

C: OK.

A: But there is an understanding that they didn't know what they were doing, or they were doing what they thought was best. They just didn't have any rules before, so they couldn't know that this room was not for bicycles.

C: So, you are not annoyed at them but it's just another responsibility, a pressure or something like that?

A: Right.

C: You have to do all the stuff …

A: Right. It's another thing to think of; to clear out and get ready, and there are so many other things that I still have to do, so …

C: What's that like for you to have a lot of things to do, a lot of pressure?

A: The way it is in the dream is not how it usually would be. So it's not going smoothly. You know, usually I would be there well ahead of time, before the participants, and everything would have been set up. So this is actually very, this is like a dream of …, an anxiety dream. Something of like, oh what would be the worst case when you have to do something, give a seminar like that. It would be that you come too late and there are already participants and you don't have time to set everything up. So that's how I am feeling, I am really feeling time pressure and uptight about this time pressure; will I manage everything in time for the beginning?

C: Where in your body do you feel this? This anxiety, this pressure?

A: In my belly area, so it's as if all the pressure is there.

C: Can you get into that a little bit more, what does that feel like?

A: It's like before a volcano erupts, or it's like a boiling pot, or a pressure cooker, so it feels like there is a lot of energy there that is still being contained but could explode easily … and it feels, mostly it feels warm in my belly, but there is a sense of, as if something is on top of it like on a pressure cooker, the top part, there is a lid on it, so it's contained.

C: Contained, but kind of volcanic, kind of you could explode.

A: Yes.

C: But it is kind of dangerous.

A: Yes.

C: Dangerous, is there an excitement there too, or is it mostly danger and fear?

A: It's not so much fear, it's more a question of will I make it in time. It is not really a fear of failure, it's more a fear of … I don't know, fear of … well, of not getting to a good start or of not getting it right from the beginning. Of looking unprofessional, or of seeming unprofessional because the start is so chaotic.

C: Tell me more about that, what would be bad about looking unprofessional?

A: Well the volunteers, the participants are applying for our organization and not only are we selecting them and deciding who goes into which project, they are also selecting us and deciding if they are going with us or a different organization or whether they are going to go to a certain country or whether they like a certain project field. [...] Here, I am the first face of the organization they meet and if they see a chaotic face then they'll just automatically think the whole, all my colleagues, the whole organization is that way. So it's not only a feeling of, that the participants will have a bad idea of how we are but they are also getting a bad idea of all my colleagues just because I didn't manage to do my job correctly.

C: OK. I hear all the pressure, all the I got to do this right for so many reasons.

A: Hmm.

C: Can you associate to where that feeling of having to do it right comes from?

A: Where that comes from? So when I have, when do I have that, or ...

C: You know, when you think of having to do it right.

A: Right.

C: What are your associations?

A: I always think, I'm sort of a perfectionist, I always think I have to do it right. So it's something that's very familiar to me. So it's like, I would say, my normal way of being. So whenever something comes that, you know in my work at least, that I have not done, prepared, because I ... I mean, anything can always come up and change things but if it's my responsibility, and I haven't prepared it well, then that's, I really have a hard time with myself. So, it almost never happens (laugh).

C: You are always so well prepared, the issue doesn't come up?

A: I try. It's hard for me if it does. It's hard for me if things don't work out as I would like them, due to my own failure. If someone else fails, that's OK but if I ... it feels like a failure if I don't plan it right. This would be, and that is why I thought it might be a good dream. This is like a situation, this would be the worst scenario I could think of at this seminar. Starting off like that would be really awful.

C: Like, can't get the lights going. I mean, these people keep interrupting ...

A: Yeah, and the chairs aren't set up, you know it's all still chaos there's no welcoming feeling to it, for the participants who are coming earlier. They are just confronted with chaos and I'm chaotic in my doing because of that. And I'm also not very welcoming because I'm so busy with all the things I still have to do. So I don't remember but I still have a sense that I tell them to take out their bikes. And I told you I wasn't annoyed with them, I could understand why they had their bikes but my voice will definitely be filled with annoyance because it's just one more thing for me to do.

C: So your voice would be kind of abrupt, kind of annoyed.

A: Yeah, they wouldn't find me a nice, interesting, (laugh) welcoming person, they would think, oh what kind of a woman is this, that would be their idea. Why is she so mad at us or why isn't she welcoming, what's her problem?

C: What's her problem, what's wrong with this woman, how come she is so abrupt and ...

A: Yeah, and also asking them to help set up the chairs. I mean in a way that's OK, it bears the sense of well that's not really that bad, I mean they are going to do a voluntary service so they might as well start right away. But on the other hand, it just seems so unprofessional, it should be different. I should have, we should have taken care of it beforehand and they shouldn't have to do anything, they should just come and learn about our program. So it's more, I see the seminar as a service to them, that we inform them, that they inform us, but not that they have to do anything, that they have to be active in helping us with the organizational part of the program.

C: This is something you should have had down pat. Everything should have been perfect by the time you get there. You should be completely in control.

A: Exactly.

C: At this point you should be welcoming them graciously…

A: Yes, yes.

C: Is there a voice in your head that you could hear when you think about: you should have this all under control, you know you should be, you said being a perfectionist is very familiar. Is there a voice you hear in your head telling you be perfect, get it all together.

A: Well there is a voice that says it's … hmm, everything else is not a possibility. So unprofessional, so it's like my standard of quality of my work is just that standard and everything below that is not allowed except maybe in really, really stressful times, I don't know in my private life or something. Overall I would say that it's part of my job to deliver that high standard and everything else is not allowed.

C: Not acceptable.

A: Not acceptable.

C: Andrea, when you hear that voice can you be that voice for a minute. Can you sound like that voice, it's not acceptable if you don't have it all together if you don't have this all organized in time. Can you say it that way?

A: Hmm. It's not acceptable, it's just out of the question, it's impossible, you have to do it this way and there's no question about it. You're not doing your job, if you don't do it in a good way.

C: Can you put a little more emotion into it?

A: Hmm. (laugh). You're a real failure if you don't do it that way, if you mess it up, if you come unprepared at the last minute, that just can't be, you're not doing your job, you shouldn't be paid, do something different. But if you do this job you have to do it in a good way, quality way. There's just no excuse for messing it up.

C: Can you be the other part of yourself now, the part that is messing up and respond?

A: Well, I know you're right but, and I know, I know, I don't understand how it could be different now but it is, something happened and this is just the way it is and I know you're upset but I can't change it. I have no idea how I got here but I can't do anything about it.

C: Can you talk about how you felt during both parts of them?

A: Well, they were both hard (laugh). Both hard to feel into. But I would say, to really feel the emotion of the high quality standard perfectionist, the unyielding sort of being, that was hard. On the other hand, the part that doesn't understand and is just feeling really awful by the situation that's also not easy to feel in there. Because it's all blocked with that not understanding.

C: Yeah. So when you finally got into it, when you were being the perfectionist, the kind of yelling at yourself, you sounded really demanding, really parental, really kind of critical and hostile.

A: Hmm.

C: Can you relate to that?

A: Yeah. There's no, it's very inflexible. There's no compassion really, it's like this is the right way and everything else is not acceptable.

C: … no compassion.

A: Yeah.

C: No excuses?

A: Yeah.

C: Then on the other side when you were apologetic you sounded defeated, you just sounded pathetic. (laugh)

A: (laugh) Yeah, it feels, that is the powerless side. Like it doesn't have any power to it.

C: It doesn't have any power?

A: Yeah, this part doesn't have any power, no. Its only way of, its only expression is not understanding and saying this is just the way it is, can't do anything. Yeah, it doesn't feel like it has any power in it.

C: Interesting you just "it" yourself at that point, right? "It doesn't have any power in it" – so you're powerless in that situation?

A: Yeah, right.

C: So it is something you don't like, so you kind of put it away from yourself.

A: Yeah it's not, I mean it's not a nice, the other feeling, or the other role, or the other part, the demanding, righteous part is very powerful. So even though it is not compassionate it feels strong. Whereas the other part just feels sort of hmm ... feels powerless, and that feeling in comparison is even worse. (laugh)

C: It's better to feel the strong.

A: Yes, unyielding sort of person, yeah ... Yeah, especially, it's really strong in the work situation.

[...]

C: So there's something about work. Do you think it is about this particular work situation, this particular job or is it kind of general?

A: No, it's coming to my mind already that this part connects to preparing for our dream session and our interview and trying to get a sense if I have prepared enough or not. And my sense is I should have done more. So it does connect to, it can connect to, well, I mean this is my private endeavor. In a way there is a professional sense to it, but I'm not being paid for it. So, I think it does also, yeah ... let me see ...

C: So go back, so you felt it strongly thinking about our session.

A: Yeah. Well I felt that connection when I was (laugh) telling you about the preparation and the chairs being set up and how it would feel to be somewhere, when I am not prepared enough. So I thought this could connect to my feeling of: am I prepared enough for talking with you?

C: Well, not knowing what to expect too, right?

A: Hmm.

C: Not something you can have all chairs set up exactly because you don't know what you are going to need ...

A: Yeah ... yeah, but there is always, you know like, hmm ... even setting up the chairs is like a minimum of what you can do and then you still don't know how it's going to work out and things and the people and the program can change and everything but it seems like setting up the chairs is just the, well like the standard first step.

C: At least you can have that.

A: Yeah.

C: Not only having, not only are the chairs not all set up, but all these bikes are all over the place

A: (laugh) Exactly.

C: And we did have some, I cancelled first and then you cancelled because you were sick. So we did have some back and forth in terms of our session.

A: Yeah, yeah we did ... I'm still a bit with that if I think it's more, I think this quality standard is very active in my working situation and I wonder, yeah I would have to, I am wondering still if it's ... I would spontaneously say I am not as unyielding or strict or even sure of what would be a high quality standard in my private life. So I would say, probably it pertains to anything where I would know what the high quality standard would be.

C: Say more about the private life part ...

A: So if I would, like, with the private life there would be things that I would say are, well, like unquestionable rules: I wouldn't lie to someone, or I wouldn't want to keep them waiting unnecessarily for me or ah, I want to be considerate or I want to help people when they are in a bad situation, or when they want to visit me I want to have time for them. Ah, or yeah, when they are in a crisis I also want to have time for them. So there are certain standards I've set for myself and I would probably be unyielding with that also. But it's, there is more of a flexibility there but you know, it's not as ..., I don't feel the pressure of it, at work I would feel the pressure of my role, I have to be true to this professional role, that's what I am being paid for, that's why I am there. And in my private life I would have to be true to my own private ideals, or my own set of rules. So they are closer to, maybe they are closer to, or they are more homegrown.

C: You've chosen them.

A: Yeah.

C: Whereas at work you feel like you have to please other people?

A: Well not, maybe it's more like it's a framework, it is just set. That's the job and those things have to be done, there is no decision about it. I mean like this selection process is, the application process, the volunteers write their applications and they have to come to the seminar and we have to make a good choice. So, that's just the framework that's set. And I'm working in that, and a lot of people are dependent on me and I know that that's the case. Yeah and in my private life I choose more, I have freedom in choosing what the framework looks like and I set the framework.

[...]

C: Let's move on to the image of the guy who appears like on TV you see his face. He wants you to send this woman out.

A: Yeah. In the dream it isn't, it's a normal phenomenon. Just when I woke up I thought, wow this is strange. I mean it's like a Harry Potter or science fiction sort of thing, 'cause he is on the floor, he is on the ground. And then there is like a circle and there is a projection of his image on the ground, just sort of comes up, as if he was phoning me. And then I see it on the ground. But it's, in the dream it is really natural to talk to him like that. So there is something about the form that's ... and I can't recall ever having dreamt something like that before, having a person talk to me in that way. It seems like an idea how future communication can be. (laugh)

C: (laugh)

A: And then he's, there is that part about not understanding exactly what he wants or what he is talking about. If I would be looking at it with my waking consciousness I would find the way that he came on the floor and he showed himself, that I would find unusual and I would expect to understand everything he says. In the dream it was the other way around. The image of him and him talking to me was really normal and not unusual at all but I couldn't understand what he was saying. He was using words, or I just didn't understand. And that was the part with the other colleague, who was annoyed that I didn't understand. But there was something, he said words but I couldn't get what he was saying.

C: And that made you anxious, like I should understand?

A: (sigh) Well it was unnerving. It was like, what is this? At first I thought this guy is just not talking clearly, but when my colleague said you know, Andrea, what is the matter with you, you should understand, it's no problem, it means that'n that'n that. I thought well maybe it was me who did not understand, you know, maybe it was my problem. But first I thought he wasn't talking clearly or coherently or ...

C: It sounds like that made you feel stupid, made you feel, like what's wrong with me?

A: Only, after the colleague said, you know, what's the matter with you? Only at that moment I thought I was, you know, I wasn't up to it. But before it was more like perplexing and irritating.

C: Yeah. And it seemed like, you said he was somehow connected to Belgian diplomacy and wanted you to send a woman out.

A: Yeah, it had the feeling, of as if this woman had an affair with the diplomat and this was causing a security problem, and that is why they wanted this woman to come outside. And right, so there was something about this woman having a relationship with the diplomat and that causing problems or security problems.

C: So they wanted you to turn her in basically.

A: Yeah, or to get her out of that situation. They didn't want her in that seminar, they didn't want her in that space. They wanted her with them.

C: She was an applicant, you said?

A: Yeah. She was an applicant.

C: They wanted to get her out so that ... somehow they wanted you to give her up.

A: Yeah.

C: What was the feeling you had when they wanted you to give her up? I mean, the colleague is saying you don't have to. One person saying you have to and the colleague saying you don't have to.

A: Well, since he is a lawyer, I felt relief. You know because first I thought we would have to do what they were saying, we were required by law to do whatever they asked us to do. And when my colleague said no, we can just ignore them, I was relieved because then I thought, OK, then we will just ignore them. They are just bluffing and we're not going to go for it. So she is an adult and she can do whatever she wants and she can be a participant in this seminar.

C: So, eventually you didn't send her out?

A: No, I didn't. No, I just didn't do anything.

C: And then the guy just disappeared.

A: Yeah, well he disappeared and then I asked my colleague what was that about and then he explained it and then the whole problem disappeared. The problem then was more the annoyance with the colleague and then he was being publicly annoyed with me so that was more of the emotional problem. But this woman sort of just was, that was over with.

C: So you said he was publicly annoyed with you, what do you mean by that?

A: Well, there were participants walking around and he just openly, you know, he didn't go to a corner or he didn't whisper, or indirectly say what he was thinking. But he was just openly annoyed with me and thought I was stupid and I thought, well you know, you don't do that in front of everyone, that's unprofessional. It's another instance of making me look bad.

C: Yeah, very much like, you know, when you played the two sides. He sounds like he was definitely the topside, top dog.

A: Yeah.

C: By being critical and hostile.

A: Yeah. He was, yeah that was, yeah no compassion, arrogant and critical. Yeah … the only good thing was that he solved the other problem …

[…]

C: Well, he is not quite honest and the guy whose image is coming and telling you something, he is not quite honest? I mean, he's telling you, you have to do something.

A: Yeah, that's true. Yeah he's bluffing. Actually the guy with the image is bluffing. He is acting like an authority figure, he's acting like he has more authority than he actually does.

C: So, can you trust these men?

A: Well the guy with the image, I don't think …, I'm sure at the beginning but at the end I think no, I can't. This colleague, hmm, it's ambivalent so there are some things I think I can trust him with and other things I have to sort of have a check, a control check, like maybe he's saying it because, or leaving something out because he wants to go in one direction and he thinks if he says everything then I'll decide another direction.

C: You can't put too much … I guess, the trust that keeps coming back, you can't trust them too much?

A: Yeah, yeah that's it.

C: And they are interfering. Here you have this seminar put together and they are interfering with your getting all those things done …

A: Well, yeah, well he's, hmm, well he does actually two things. On the one hand he helps me because he gets rid of this problem so it is solved really easily. 'Cause I don't have to worry about it anymore. On the other hand he creates another problem that of being annoyed with me so publicly. So it's both, it has one of relief and one of extra annoyance.

[…]

C: … these kids, well it is kind of interesting, there is a lot about relationships here that, these kids you could ask them to help you and they should be volunteering to help you. But you are also supposed to be professional and have everything ready, so they shouldn't have to help you.

A: Right.

C: There's kind of lots of conflict in your relationships …

A: Hmm. Yeah and ambivalence. In a sense there it's OK to ask them and in another sense it's not OK. But it's, I mean there is a hierarchy, it would be worse not to have the chairs set up.

C: Hmm.

A: So it's better to ask them to help and then we have everything set up than to not ask and not have it ready on time.

C: Right. So that kind of wins out, that being on time, that having everything ready to go is more important than having, than asking, the fear of asking for help.

A: Yeah, yeah.

[…]

C: … Kind of sounds like there is some flux in your life. Kind of time when you are not absolutely sure what you are going to do.

A: Yeah, that's true, that's true.

[...]

C: Andrea, I was thinking, why don't we take like a 5-minute break? And then we can move on to the insight stage, sound good?

A: Yeah, sounds good.

The insight stage

C: Can you talk about how are you feeling right now about the whole process?

A: I am enjoying it very much. I really appreciate it and it always amazes me again and again, how much is in a dream.

C: Yes, how quickly it gets to all the important issues.

A: Yeah. (laugh)

C: So, Andrea, at this point right now what do you think the dream means?

A: I think there might be several dimensions to it. One would be giving me a picture of the anxiety that I felt preparing for this session and the interview with you. ... What it also dips into the whole part about, specifically this seminar, and the pressure that I put myself under, or that is there, and that I add to, maybe by that unyielding perfectionism. And the part about what do I do with situations where I am not living up to my high quality standards ... (sigh) Also about the question about trusting and not trusting and figuring out other people. What you summarized, the ambivalence within relationships in general, asking for help or thinking it's not professional to ask for help. So the question how can I fill the role I am playing and actually who is defining it? Is it really defined, like in the work situation I would say it is defined by the framework, and I think the question arises whether that really is true. (pause) Yeah.

C: Sounds like you have a really good handle on it.

A: Yes.

C: Which is very cool.

A: (laugh)

C: One thing I thought we could do in terms of the insight stage would be to do a little bit more about a kind of a "parts of self" type thing. Where we take this guy, who was the image – what part of you is he like. You talked about him as, hmm, he was critical, he was demanding, he was bluffing, he was trying to get something he wanted from you, he was a little unclear – he was using words you couldn't quite understand … I wonder, what part of you is like that, he kind of appears as an image?

A: (sigh) Well it would be a part that seems very distant, like a projection. I don't feel a strong connection to it, it comes out of the blue, pops up and says something and then sort of goes away. It acts like it has a lot of power. So the way it comes is the distance and in the not understanding there is also a distance in it. It would be a part that I'm not familiar with, that seems foreign. I can't get a grip on it, it just comes and goes, but while it's there it seems more real than it is.

C: What part of you is like that? Are there some situations where you are like that? Where you withdraw, you are distant, don't connect as much?

A: It's like when I am in my analytical thinking mode, not connected to the rest of my emotions or body sensations or feelings. I am distant from the rest of me, but it seems like it is all of me. I've done a lot of Focusing and looked into my dreams and I learned to integrate other dimensions and to sense into there. But I go into the thinking mode easily. When I am more in my body, and I can do that more easily now than I used to, this thinking mode seems distant.

C: That's interesting. Kind of just the image that you are just the head …

A: Exactly. (laugh) Just the head and the idea that it's all, and powerful, and says everything.

C: It's a masculine side ...

A: Yeah, and it's interesting that I don't understand it. The perspective has turned. I would still say, even though I've done a lot of Focusing and working on my dreams ... my default state of being is thinking, especially in stressful situations I would go there right away, but in the dream it's showing me the other way around.

C: Hmm. It's interesting in the dream, the message from your colleague is you don't have to pay attention to that side.

A: (laugh) Yeah. At least it's not as powerful as I imagine it to be. But he also doesn't understand why I don't understand it.

C: So let's go to the colleague. What part of you is like this lawyer colleague, you talked about him as strategic, you worked well together with him, he's stern and judging, strategic, you don't quite trust him, what part of you is like that?

A: (sigh). That's harder. Because the part where he is not open and honest and doesn't say things because he is strategic, that is something I wouldn't want to own. (laugh) So it makes it more difficult to think of it as a part of me. Hmm ... In a way it's similar to the image, it's the part that recognizes that there is a deeper felt sense of the situation, it knows that, but it acts like it's not there. So I would say it's the part that's on the lookout for sensing into negative emotions, that doesn't want to go there. It's strategic in the way that it doesn't want me to go to the sensations and feelings that might depress me, or worry me. So it only tries to stay with the rules, the regulations, the lawyer sort of thing, the framework, the things that are already clear as a guide and not all that complicated chaotic, emotional stuff.

C: Hmm. So I am struck by that these two characters in the dream are men. In your perception what are women compared to these two men?

A: Well men stand for the power play, the strategic thinking, rules and regulation. Women are more for the emotional side, for the creative side, or for the flexible side, being more in life and not about life. It makes sense that they are both the power players, the strategic thinkers, arrogant ones (laugh) that bluff their way through life. They are not so "down to earth," or authentic, or caring or compassionate.

[...]

C: It's all related to this seminar, the applicants who are idealistic, where you send people to other countries to help promote peace, right?

A: Right.

C: What part do you think that plays in the whole thing? Here you are selecting applicants for this peaceful mission, what role does that play?

A: Hmm ... One part is actually about issues I have with that seminar and with work. And another part might be it's the beginning of something. It's a seminar which makes a big decision about the future life of many of them.

[...]

C: I guess the whole is also about can we have peace? Can we communicate? What kind of relationship can we have with people?

A: Yeah. That's the issue with the seminar, the value judgments you have to make and how can you make them in a good way, peaceful, compassionate way, that is respectful as much as it can be.

C: It talks a lot about your values and about how you want to lead your life.

A: Yes. On the surface it's all about getting the rooms organized. What comes up now is that I moved into my new apartment, and I still have to get the rooms organized and prepared (laugh). Another dimension. It's pointing more to the beginning of a process, like the selection process is the beginning for the people we take on and it's the beginning of the seminar.

C: It's also the beginning of a way of life ...

A: Yeah. Maybe …

C: You said the surface is getting the rooms organized, what is the depth?

A: Well the depth would be the value or the value questions.

C: OK, right. How you want to live your life?

A: Yeah.

C: Can you go into that depth level a little more, just talk a little bit more about how do you want to live your life, what are your values right now, who are you? Big questions.

A: (laugh). Yes very big questions. With work it's what do I want to do, how much risk am I willing to take to give my passion more room, working with dreams. […] Also how much is life serious, or play or a combination of both. That is a more recent issue. Maybe I am too serious about everything. That fits into that framework, that rigidity and unyielding idea of how it should be. And play, is more it can be different, and try it out and not taking everything so seriously.

C: Two sides, the serious side, the masculine, you've got to get ahead, you have to be perfect, follow all the rules. Then there is this playful side, have fun, get into your dreams, kind of let your passions go.

A: Yeah. And trust in those in the energy that you get from that.

C: It is a dilemma. (laugh)

A: (laugh) Yeah.

C: If you imagine yourself 30 years from now. How would you like to be remembered?

A: (sigh) Hmm. Well, it comes really fast two answers. (laugh) One is how other people would remember me, and one is how I would like to look back.

C: Oh, OK. Good.

A: The one how others would remember me, sides with the work I've been doing, because it's for a good cause and we need a lot of that. If I would be working with dreams I would get a lot of ambivalent reactions to that. But on the other hand, for me, I would want to look back at the end of my life; I would have wanted me to find a way to live my passionate side.

C: Hmm. That's interesting. When you project forward, what you want is to be able to say, I did the things I wanted to do, I followed my dream.

A: Yeah.

C: ... Andrea, I know we could go with this for long, but could you summarize what you think now the dream means, or the most salient thing you'll take out with you?

A: Now I have more of a sense of the feeling I had in the dream, the time pressure, of getting the rooms ready. So it's about clearing the space in my new apartment, and looking for the chairs to put up and asking for help and sensing into that. I am not at the place I wanted but I can still do it. Sense of urgency, sense of action actually (I know we're coming to the action stage) that comes with that, that comes with the dream, the sense of being active and preparing and the urgency in that.

The action stage

C: Feeling like you need to make some changes in your life and this is a time to be thinking about it?

A: Sort of like clearing or preparing space. Finally finishing off taking all the books out of the boxes. Clearing a space to be able to write my book well. Thinking more about what it means to prepare the space to be able to start.

C: That's interesting, I like that. So kind of preparing your space mentally and physically so that you can go to this next step of doing what you want to do.

A: Yeah. Yeah. And the interconnecting rooms and finding the space where I want to talk, it is still at the point before it starts. So it is still searching for the good point of how to start. And that pressure, it's really time to do something.

C: It's interesting you said that the applicants are beginning and what you are saying now, you are identifying with them, really. You are starting, you're beginning. You have to figure out where you want to speak from. Where your voice is going to come from.

A: Yeah. Exactly.

C: How do you get organized and find your voice.

A: Yeah. Yes. …

C: Love that metaphor. (laugh)

A: (laugh) Yes it is wonderful.

C: How would you change the dream? You could do anything you want, it's your dream?

A: Oh, I would have it all set up already. (laugh)

C: OK. Say more.

A: All that chaos, I would want that to be gone. I would love to have some magic and just go click my fingers and it would all be set and ready and I would even have time to go for a walk before the program starts. I would be all at ease, in a good mood and a lot of humor, welcoming these applicants. That would be the best to find a really easy, fast way to clear up the situation and have a break. (laugh)

C: You sound even more relaxed even when you say it.

A: Yes. (laugh)

C: You click the fingers, it would all be set up, you would go for a walk, you kind of get centered, figure out what you want, you are at ease, you have humor, you'd be welcoming, you'd be generous, open.

A: Exactly.

C: You could focus on … I remember what you said: "I don't want to do this again, I don't want that chaos, I don't want that pressure, that horrendous feeling."

A: Yeah. (sigh) That's true. I would also change the structure of the place. I would want it to be one big space. Now it is not connected, it's not clear, it's all jumbled up.

C: Good. So you want one big space, all connected, all clear, open. Where would the mike be?

A: (laugh) Well if there is one space and it is all open I don't need a mike, I could talk on my own.

C: Oh, that's great, your voice is loud enough, your voice can carry.

A: Right, exactly.

C: You have a voice.

A: Yes, yes.

C: You just have to find the environment for the voice to fit in.

A: Right, exactly. (laugh)

C: The building, you said before it was a bungalow, this temporary disconnected place. What would the building itself look like?

A: It would be a lot nicer, a big room, a high ceiling, maybe even an older house, but with a big room, a warm room, with wood.

C: … inviting …

A: Yes, an inviting place, which is not old and stuffy. It would be warm, transparent and inviting.

C: How would you be dressed? You didn't talk about that before, but how would you in this room, this warm inviting room, with lots of windows, high ceilings, lots of wood, how would you be dressed?

A: I would like to be dressed in something that's very comfortable but still a bit unconventional. Something that is not tight or scratchy. It's very comfortable but still there would be something unusual about it, like maybe an unusual structure or an unusual color combination. Something that is nice to look at, catches your eye, but for me, feeling it from the inside, it fits, it's comfortable.

C: I get an image of something kind of flowing, not tailored. Something comfortable, but where people would notice you and say: "oh, she's kind of artistic." Is it an artistic look kind of?

A: Yeah. But the form doesn't have to be artistic, because with artistic clothing I imagine something uncomfortable. (laugh) The form can be clear, it doesn't have to be unusual. I think it's more a question of the pattern or the color combination.

C: Hmm. The thing you would notice first is that it looks a bit unusual but comfortable. It sounds like it really is an expression of who you are?

A: Yeah... that probably is true. (laugh)

C: So, Andrea, how can you make this happen? (laugh)

A: (laugh)

C: What you want is to be peaceful, to be yourself, look like yourself, to be comfortable, to be able to have your voice, to be able to be in a space that is clear and like you where you can work and where you can be yourself. How can you make all that happen?

A: Well I would say it's pointing to the dream passion side of work and doing something to make that possible – in a way like today, reserving the day for the book project and really taking my time, even though I have a special visitor. This might be conflicting, but saying no, this is my priority, this is important to me ... To stay with that idea, you know when I said, that is not a part that I can easily identify with, this colleague who is being strategic and just showing some parts and not everything – I just had the idea, that is more or less what I do in my work. In comparison to other people, I am authentic, I can be who I am. It's not like my dream passion – everyone knows about it – but it doesn't have a space. It could be integrated into the work but it is not. So there is a part of me that I don't use there, and there are some things I don't say because I feel that it wouldn't fit – that's not the sort of person that should work there. So with my work there is that strategic way of, maybe of acting, not saying some things because I think they don't fit in.

C: So you would like to be more authentic?

A: Yeah. To take more of a risk, and maybe to just see what happens.

C: Just be who you are.

A: Yeah.

C: And that's just who you are. (laugh)

A: (laugh) yeah.

C: That sounds really strong, that wanting to be more authentic, want to take more risks, want to be more organized, want to have more of your clean unchaotic space …

A: Hmm. (sigh)

C: Just very practically what would be your first step?

A: I had to order a desk, because I didn't have a desk for my computer, on which I could write my book, because I knew I needed a good space to write. Now I have to clear out the room of boxes and everything that is in there. So that would be a concrete next step, and the dream sort of brings with it the urgency of that. Sort of like, you put it off now for so many weeks, now it's time to act.

C: Hmm. It sounds like you feel fairly confident that you could do that once you make that decision.

A: Yeah. I think before my visitors came, I decided I had to clear up and organize a big part of the apartment and I managed that. So I know I can do it if I really put my mind to it. (laugh)

C: What are the barriers, what has kept you from doing that?

A: (sigh) Well, hmm, other priorities or the usual excuses, coming home from work and thinking, well you know, you worked the whole day so now you can just relax, read a book, and you'll do it tomorrow. That helps with the dream, having the sense of the time pressure and the urgency. Having the visitors helped, because

I knew they were coming and before they came, I wanted to have the rooms set up. It is like the dream is giving me a visitor that is coming and the urgency of that, and the idea that the program is going to start in a very short time and I have to move.

C: Hmm. Yeah. That sense of urgency if this is something you want. Yet the program starting is something external, what I am hearing is that you have to make it something internal. From what you are saying, it is not like something else is starting, if you want this book to happen, you have to make it happen.

A: Right.

C: You have to make it an internal kind of thing.

A: Right.

C: Because nobody is going to come to your door and say that you have to have this book written by a certain amount of time.

A: No, but what helped me in the other situations was having such an external push, right. So, even though I am the one who wants to write the book, I think it would help me to push me to do it by having a … like this dream is almost like it is an externalized reason.

C: So even if it would be hard on your own to set a priority of this is something so I am going to do it. By having the dream you can say, "the dream told me to do it."

A: Yeah, (laugh) exactly. The dream told me it's really urgent now, there is time pressure. I know there is pressure, but I wouldn't have said it is that urgent. So the dream is making it more clear and urgent.

C: I guess I would like to, from a therapeutic standpoint, would like to hear you say: "I choose to make more important, this is my priority, this is what I want to."

A: Right. Right. (laugh)

C: So you take complete ownership.

A: Yeah, yeah. Well I think writing the book, choosing to write the book and making that the priority, that is not the problem. That is something I want to do and choose to do. It's probably this old child conflict with cleaning up a room, or making order. This inner conflict, you know, of why is that needed, can't we do that tomorrow … I think it is connected to that in some way. It's like the outer circumstances of clearing the space, the inner drive of wanting to write the book and being motivated to write the book and read about it, that is all there, but creating the outer space to do it, that is somehow blocked.

C: That's where you get stuck?

A: Yeah.

C: This all interacts with your job, so how do you work all that out?

A: (Deep sigh and long pause). Good question. (laugh)

C: (laugh) … and the answer is not so easy …

A: (laugh) Yeah.

C: Well you talk about getting organized, clearing space for you to have your voice, how do you do that at your job?

A: When I decided to write the book, well the decision is older, but last fall I decided to work less, to work four days a week, so I would have more time to write the book. Because I realized if I have a full-time job it would be really hard to do that. So, one step was to make more room, create more time for writing. Another idea was to go part time with my work and build up like a dream counseling practice on the side. Now, the clear part is writing the book and trying to finish it by the fall. The part that is not clear is when to go part time. Because starting October I am working full time again. So it is a question of talking to my boss. I have told him that is what I want to do, but we haven't become concrete in how can we make that possible and when. That is actually connected to this selection seminar. My first idea had been to stop, to go part time and I wouldn't have to do it again next year. Now, I am unsure if that is realistic, or if I have to do it one more time and then go part time. So that is where I am at workwise.

C: Well, let me tell you my fantasy, which is – you said, you know, you wanted some magic, you wanted to be able to just click your fingers and have it all set up. What I wonder is, can you do that, can you figure out some way to get someone hired to help you.

A: Hmm.

C: Somebody, you know, so you could click your fingers and say, "go do it."

A: Yeah.

C: So you don't have to do it all.

A: (pause) Yeah, get more help, yeah.

C: I love the idea of the magic of clicking your fingers and getting someone else to do it. (laugh)

A: (good hearty laugh)

C: So that you can do the more important parts of it.

A: Yeah.

C: I mean, do you have to be organizing the chairs?

A: (long laugh). Yeah. (pause) Yeah, that is a good question. Yeah, that links to a lot of places – that asking for help and the question is that professional or not. And sometimes not realizing that it is possible to ask for help. Yeah.

C: Good thing that asking for help. (laugh)

A: (laugh) Yeah.

C: I was thinking of, as you were talking, there was a really powerful book, it always served me as a huge metaphor for my life. There was a woman, can't remember if she was in her thirties or forties, she took off six months and she went to Nantucket during the winter.

A: Hmm.

C: There were no people around, she was in an isolated place, she had a dog. And every day she got up and said: "what do I want to do?" The whole notion of centering herself and trying to figure out what do I want to do.

A: Hmm.

C: It helped her change her life. I am using that as a metaphor, because it seems that is where you are.

A: Right.

C: Trying to figure out what do I want.

A: Yeah.

C: Not what does everybody else want. Not what is everybody else going to think, but what do I want. What do I want today, right now? Is it to get organized and get your desk and books set up or is it to take care of yourself in some other way? I don't know what the most important thing is. For you to be able to feel comfortable, dressing the way you want, setting your priorities, figuring out who you are ... it is such an audacious thing, right?

A: Yeah. (Pause) Actually, I know the word audacious but I am not sure what it means.

C: Bold, taking a risk. (laugh) But as a good metaphor: "I don't know what audacious means," that is very good!

A: (hearty and long laugh) Yeah, that is true. That is good. (sigh)

C: So what have you learned about yourself?

A: Oh, a lot. (pause) I'll start at the end because that was now so clear, there is some inner urgency, not the time pressure – the external one. There is an inner urgency to clear that space and make the writing possible. I haven't sensed into that inner urgency of doing that enough. So I have learned about that. Also the part about, the hard part about owning that part of myself that looks like the colleague, and recognizing that is me at my workplace. I really like ... well, first I thought, what a question, "what do I want to wear?" but then I really liked what came. So that image of how I would look and actually how easy it was to say what I wanted, what I wanted to be different and how that connected to the question of asking for help. (pause) That sense of preparing a beginning, of being at a point in my lifetime where I am at a beginning, or am preparing something that is beginning, or I am preparing a decision to begin something or not. I knew about that, but I feel when it connects to the dream images or the dream story it gets a different

C: ... because it is coming from you ...

A: Yeah. It feels connected in a different way, hmm. It feels like it's its own gestalt, it is not only my thinking about it but it is my whole body, all my sensations, or felt senses about it, it seems more like all of it.

C: One of the things I am struck by is the whole person-centered kind of notion. I was just reading a chapter that Art Bohart wrote. He talks about the client being a self-healer.

A: Yeah.

C: How, that is just so true, I think that is the real beauty of client-centered stuff that it all comes from you.

A: Yeah.

C: It's nothing that anybody else can or should ever tell you. The whole dream is about you, and what do you want, and what do you need, and what are your priorities. So it is really a nice dream for a person-centered approach, right? (laugh)

A: (laugh) Yeah. That's why I think the two go together so well. I have a sense of dreaming being also a self-healing process ...

C: Yes, absolutely. You got to pay attention to them to find out what it is you need.

A: Exactly. Exactly. So sometimes a wound might be there, that needs more attention than just healing by itself. And then you look at it or you sense into it. Yeah.

C: The other thing that is interesting is at the beginning you talked about you were kind of disappointed that it wasn't a bigger dream. And when you look at this dream it really is a big dream.

A: Yeah. Yeah. That's what I have recognized often working on dreams with partners, but it is so ingrained. Oh, thinking, this is about work and I don't want to think about that now, or it's not like flying or something spectacular.

C: Perfect.

A: Yeah. (laugh)

The client's summary

Almost three hours of dreamsensing can give a good impression of the multidimensionality and complexity of one dream. The first exploration stage revealed the anxiety and urgency dimension inherent in the dream and its waking life connection to preparing for the dream session itself. Another waking life connection was the realization that I add to the pressure that is involved in the seminar at work by letting my perfectionism and high quality standard rule. Dimensions of other waking life situations where I do not live up to my high-quality standards opened up. The dreamsensing also brought up questions of my trusting or not trusting other people and trying to figure them out. My ambivalence within relationships and the idea that asking for help is unprofessional were touched upon. Lastly the dreamsensing brought up the question of how I fill the roles I am playing at my work and who defines them.

The insight stage brought more depth to many of these issues. By sensing into the dream characters as parts of myself I realized that both the masculine characters, the "image of the head on the floor" of the dream – the analytical, stern, heady part of me – and the colleague – the strategic, following the rules, "don't go into chaotic emotional stuff" – part of me – are power players, partly arrogant and bluffing their way. I made the connection between my current life situation and the situation of the seminar participants: being at the beginning of something, preparing a decision to change life radically. It brought up the question of values and how I want to live my life: is it more playful or more serious, should I do work that I am passionate about or work that has a peaceful, world changing mission. I felt in more depth the sense of urgency in the dream of being active, getting the rooms ready in time, getting organized, clearing a space.

In the last stage, the action stage, I elaborated the next steps that follow out of all that came up in the dreamsensing in the prior two stages. What concrete steps can I take to clear the space needed to write my book? What can lead me in seeking and organizing a good place from which to speak and find my voice? Another dimension of the "colleague" part of me arose, when I realized that I am sometimes like that in my work, weighing what to say strategically. Taking a step away from that would mean to take more risks, be more authentic and see what happens. Clearer also was the idea that a further step might be to ask for help, or even to realize that it is possible to get help.

Differentiating the dream sessions: A client's perspective

Of course the experience of dreamsensing was different with each dream and with each approach. Needless to say, it makes a substantial difference if one has an hour for a dream session or three. Also, there is a difference in talking with someone face to face or on the phone. Yet I think there are more significant differences that are not so closely linked to these context issues. What is striking is the difference in the pace of the process. Focusing organically brings with it a slowness, a pausing, a taking of time to sense within. I was also Focusing as well in the other two sessions, usually where there were pauses or where I was prompted to sense within. Also evident is that I came out of the sessions with an understanding linked to different levels of insight connected to experiential, emotional and/or cognitive levels of meaning.

I find the integrative model on insight that Pascual-Leone and Greenberg (2007) developed to be very helpful when trying to understand what happened in the three sessions from the client's perspective. They differentiate between different levels of abstraction and processing and they place the differing theoretical therapeutic orientations (experiential-humanistic/psychoanalytical/ cognitive behavioral) on a continuum:

> We suggest an integrative model of insight based on two dimensions: the degree of abstraction (abstracting from within a single situation vs. across different types of situations) and the type of processing (perceptual-emotional vs. rational-conceptual). This theoretical conceptualization helps delineate characteristics of the three processes of awareness, meta-awareness, and conceptual linking. Thus, qualitatively different processes of insight are understood as falling on a continuum from experience-near (i.e., emotional awareness and a more existential meta-awareness) to experience-far (i.e., linking pieces of knowledge into conceptual formulations). (p. 52)

Considering these two dimensions and placing the dream sessions within them, I would situate the session with McGavin at one end of the continuum, i.e., experience-near, with a low level of abstraction and with more of a perceptual-emotional type of processing.

> From an experiential perspective, meaning is best constructed by exploring specific situations in depth to discover what one is, in fact, experiencing. Clients are better able to "taste" their immediate experience by exploring a single experience in depth, subsequently, clients make use of an inherent, spontaneous, and adaptive self-organizing process to promote survival and growth. (Ibid., p. 42)

With both Lemke and Hill similar experience-near insights were attained. Yet they also guided me to more abstract levels of conceptual processing including linking insights.

> When linking occurs in experiential therapies it comes without explicit interpretation. It is constructed bottom-up by the client rather than being offered by the therapist, which would necessarily involve more top-down processing by the client. Thus, *experiential linking*, which unfolds spontaneously from some clients, is a form of insight that is high in abstraction while still in the purview of perceptual-emotional processing. (Ibid., p. 43)

What differentiates the three processes, then, is what my attention was focused on. With McGavin my awareness was focused on my immediate moment-by-moment (bodily) unfolding of experience. Whereas with Lemke and Hill I dipped into this level and then out of it, attending more to linking my experiencing with other similar situations in waking life or with different aspects of myself. With Hill I also sensed explicitly into the future, searching for the "right" next action steps to take. With Lemke and McGavin these next steps and areas of change that would come after the dream session were more implicit.

I came to all three dream sessions with an intention of finding a deeper meaning to my dreams. The path I followed with each led me to various levels of insight into the meaning of the dream. With Lemke it felt like a dipping in and out of the dream experience, being led by the evolving dream story from beginning, middle to end. It was as if we paused at each turn of the dream path to consider the dream self and how it experiences itself in relation to the other dream characters, and then sensing if this relates to particular waking life situations. With McGavin it felt more like finding the "pregnant" spot and then going deeper and deeper in experiencing and bodily felt meaning. With Hill the path could develop longer and thus encompass more than with the others. The exploration of the dream experiencing was more thorough and detailed, the insights gathered could connect to more waking life issues and the action steps found sketched a more explicit future path.

When viewing the three dream narratives in progression – as a "mini dream series" spanning a time frame of five months – it becomes clear that some issues are touched upon in each dream. One example of this is the inner conflict between the "top dog" perfectionist – not wanting to go to the dark, emotional stuff – and the "underdog" – which is more of a bodily sense, not yet very articulate. In addition, this could be seen as a mirror image of a conflict on a more general level in my life, of whether to give dreams and the dreaming life more and more room in my own life.

Guiding Through
the Territory

After having shared the experiencing of three dream sessions in Chapter 3 and having considered the perspective of the client, it is time to sense into the perspective of the therapist. In all three of the dream sessions the therapist/guide moved along the empathic path sketched in Chapter 2. They each collaborated with the client in a creative endeavor. Each dreamsensing was a creative meaning-making process with the concomitant "aha" moments and revelations signaled by a spoken word "right," or a sigh or laughter etc. Aside from being a confident companion, accompanying the client in a person-centered way, what else did each therapist specifically add and what aspect of experiencing did they guide or particularly attend to? I want to start with Hill's model, the most structured and elaborate of the three, because it offers a framework in which to place the other two approaches. This will make it easier to compare the three approaches and point to their similarities and differences. In the end I will offer some ideas about choosing the "right" path in guiding through the dreamsensing territory.

Dream work in therapy: Facilitating exploration, insight, and action

This subheading is the title of Clara Hill's book (2004) where she gives a thorough description of her three-stage model of working with dreams. She considers her model to be cognitive-experiential, cognitions and emotions being worked on throughout the model. The theoretical foundation of the first (exploration) stage is explicitly client-centered, as she notes, "The provision of empathy and collaboration and the belief that the client is self-healing make this stage (and the whole model) client-centered" (p. 7). In the other two stages she has integrated ideas of psychodynamic dream theory. Her conception of the action stage was also influenced by the ideas of behavioral theorists. Hill developed the structural framework within her approach specifically in order to be able to do therapy research on her model, which also required that it needed to be easily taught to others. Obviously Hill wants her model to be used as a guideline and the structure is there for orientation, being of particular help when first learning the skills needed with dreamsensing.

In the initial *exploration stage*, the client first retells the dream in first-person present tense. The client is then asked to explore her overall feelings ("the emotional climate of the dream") and if the client hasn't mentioned it yet, to say when the dream occurred. Subsequently, the client chooses three to five images to sense into more thoroughly. The therapist guides the exploration of the images – in the sequence they occurred in the dream – by using the following mnemonic coined by Hill to remember the different steps:

a. **D**escription
b. **R**e-experiencing feelings
c. **A**ssociations
d. **W**aking life triggers

At the end of this stage it might be helpful for the therapist to ask for or offer a summary. "In the exploration stage, the therapist serves as a coach, helping the client explore the dream images. The therapist avoids having expectations about what content will emerge but focuses instead on guiding the exploration process" (ibid., p. 19). The dream session in Chapter 3 gives a good impression of this first stage. Usually though, this stage would not take as long. The model is conceived of as taking a time span of 60 to 90 minutes for the whole session, with the exploration stage taking up about half of the session and the latter two stages each a quarter.

Within the next stage, the *insight stage*, after having asked the client for her initial understanding of the dream, Hill suggests constructing the meaning of the dream on several possible levels of insight:

1. Experience: going into the dream experience in more depth
2. Waking life: seeking insights connected to waking life issues (past, present or future)
3. Inner personality dynamics: (a) parts of self; (b) conflicts originating in childhood; (c) spiritual/existential

In the dream session in Chapter 3 Hill suggested beginning with sensing into the level of inner personality dynamics, specifically the "parts of self." Jung developed the idea that dream characters can either stand for themselves or for some part of the dreamer. Gestalt therapists went one step further in suggesting that all parts of the dream can be considered as parts of oneself (including inanimate parts). Hill cautions: "Because the idea of dreams representing parts of the self is an unfamiliar concept to many people, some rationale and education are often needed for why the therapist thinks that a parts-of-self focus is appropriate" (2004, p. 53) (see also the related concept of "self-dialogues" or "configurations of self" as developed by Mearns and Thorne, 2007). In my dream session Hill dipped into this way of sensing once during that first exploration stage, when she asked me as the client to be the part that is judgmental and annoyed and to be the other part it was in conflict with, the part that felt like it had caused the problem. Though my example arose earlier in the session, Hill mentions the possibility of using this "two-chair exercise" particularly during the insight stage (originally from Gestalt therapy, Greenberg and others have integrated this exercise in their process experiential approach, see Purton, 2004). When an inner conflict arises while sensing into the "parts of self" insight level, this exercise can help the client to explore and understand her conflict more experientially. Hill recommends that the client is asked to summarize her insights at the end of this stage in order to consolidate what she has learned about the dream.

During the last stage, *the action stage*, the therapist aids the client in considering what she has learned so far from the previous stages of dreamsensing and how that might translate into concrete changes in her waking life. Hill emphasizes that clients differ greatly in how much input they need from the therapist in this stage. "Some clients spontaneously move to action after the insight stage ... Other clients, however, need more help moving on to the action stage ... either they need someone to provide an opportunity for them to think about action, or they need someone to suggest ideas for action, or they need someone to teach them specific skills" (2004, p. 71).

In the action stage Hill suggests three possible steps:

A. Ask client to change the dream or create a sequel
  1. In fantasy
  2. During sleep

B. Coach client about making changes in waking life
  1. Specific behavioral change
  2. Ritual to honor the dream
  3. Continued working with dreams

C. Ask client to summarize action plan

The major philosophical underpinning of the action stage is that clients are the active agents of their own lives. ... The role of the helper in this stage is to serve as a coach, cheerleader, supporter, information-giver, and consultant, but not to take over and "fix" the client. This stage, then, is still client-centered, with helpers facilitating clients in thinking about change rather than imposing change on them. (Hill, 2009, p. 290)

The relational person-centered approach

Lemke stands for what I have termed the relational person-centered approach. The essential guiding principle of the session is developing and maintaining a high-quality therapeutic relationship (or to put it differently, working at "relational depth", see Mearns and Cooper, 2005). Specifically for sensing into dreams the parallel question might be phrased as: "What is the dream telling the dreamer?" Lemke posits three possible ways of helping the client find an understanding of her dream:

- Supporting (emotionally) the finding of associations to the dream metaphors and symbols
- Helping recall memories connected with the symbol and helping to place these in the dreamer's personal and social context
- Giving one's own associations to symbols in order to stimulate the process (rather than an interpretation, which might generate resistance on the part of the client)

Lemke uses all of these three ways during the dream session in Chapter 3. Initially she tries to guide me as the client to associations concerning the place of the dream, the museum. When that does not bring up much, she starts to guide the client through the dream, stopping to view each dream character as a symbol of a part of the self. The process thus consisted of asking for associations and feelings, guiding the client to link it with situations in waking life and every now and then giving her own associations to certain parts of the dream. When compared to the stages in the Hill model, it seems that Lemke moves back and forth between exploration of the dream and insight, interweaving exploration and insight. In her book Lemke has examples of working on all of the various levels that Hill mentions for the insight stage. When it comes to the action stage, this is more implicit with Lemke than with Hill. There is a trust in the development of the client, that she will change her life and her behavior according to the insights gained in the therapy session.

Focusing and dreamsensing

The dream session with McGavin is in some ways strikingly different from the other two. Even though there has been a considerable theoretical discussion on whether Focusing is or is not to be considered person-centered (see, for example, Purton, 2004 or Thorne, 2003), I doubt that anyone would challenge, that McGavin's very close following of the client's unfolding experiencing is person-centered. This orientation stems partly from her developing – together with Ann Weiser Cornell – a specific form of Focusing called "Inner Relationship Focusing" (Weiser Cornell, 2005). Inner Relationship Focusing enhances the client's own person-centered way of being with her inner world or inner felt sensings and aids the client in becoming more finely aware and in touch with the particulars of her own experiencing. This process entails sensing into different parts within as well as finding ways to keep company with sometimes very divergent parts, including parts that are seemingly in conflict. It increases the unconditional regard towards all that arises and expands the client's self-empathy, essential qualities for sensing into dreams.

Relating the dream session with McGavin to the Hill model, one could say that both the exploration stage and the action stage are – if at all – only implicitly present. Almost all of the session is about experiencing in depth a part of the dream – in this case the part where the dreamer and dream disagree. This would correlate with Hill's "the experience itself" level of insight:

> Rather than thinking of the dream as reflecting something else, it can be understood in terms of the experience itself. … The dream is an experience that the client lived through, albeit during sleep rather than waking life, and thus is important in and of itself. In this case, the dream does not need to be "interpreted"; rather, it needs to be experienced and understood for what it is. By examining this level, clients can learn more about the depths of their wishes, desires, fears, doubts, and feelings. (Hill, 2004, p. 49)

Pascual-Leone and Greenberg point to what kinds of challenges this sensing into (the dream as an) experience itself can bring to the therapist accompanying such a process:

> Experiential awareness is neither associative linking nor the uncovering of meaning, rather, it is the progressive cocreation of meaning in a single moment as a therapist facilitates the elaboration of a client's ongoing experience. … The experiential therapist is continually confronted by the elusiveness and complexity of a client's emotion that results from its spontaneous, changing, and very subjective nature. Therefore, facilitating insight in an experiential framework requires a great deal of tentativeness on the part of the therapist. This means that the therapist must handle the client's emerging awareness in a manner that is non-content-directive and exploratory, rather than prescriptive. … Therapists must rely on clients themselves as the main source

of material from which insights stem. In experiential therapies, the client (rather than the therapist) is the original author of any insight. Thus, the therapist has the precarious job of helping the client discover something that the therapist is not privy to. (2007, pp. 47–48)

In a Focusing process both the guide and the client are Focusing. The slow motion of the process can enhance the understanding of the therapist on a bodily level, while the client comes closer to the bodily re-experiencing of the dream. In addition – for both the guide and the client – practicing Focusing anchors the inner sense of the "right" pace, of taking the time needed and staying patient enough to let something evolve from within. On a more general level, Focusing can enhance any path of dreamsensing; both Hill (1996, pp. 41–42) and Lemke (2000, p. 15) mention the significance of Gendlin's work on dreams.

Diverging pathways?

The three approaches share a person-centered way to dreamsensing, and yet they also are, in some aspects, very different. They differ in how much and in what ways they are structured and by what they are structured: Hill uses the structure of the process as a defining part of her model; Lemke structures her dream sessions according to the quality of the relationship and also in a following of the dream story; McGavin structures the dream session with the intention of deepening and supporting the experiential process, sometimes specifically in a place where dream and dreamer disagree. They also differ in the pace they set, with Focusing at one end of the continuum, in its setting of a very slow and tentative pace. Another difference emerges according to what needs to be especially attended to, that is, where the understanding or insights come from. With McGavin the understanding primarily sought is an experiential one, with both Lemke and Hill the understanding lies within the linking of emotional and cognitive insights.

Whereas Hill explicitly stresses the importance of the last stage leading to the client's formulation of concrete action steps, in the other approaches action steps and behavioral changes are implicit in the process and are believed to arise organically after the dream session. While "action" is not a word usually found in person-centered literature it points to the more general question of how "active" the therapist should or can be. In Chapter 2 I have pointed to the issue of safety brought up by the special territory of dreamsensing. I agree with Mearns (2003, p. 82) who states that one of the most important points about person-centered work is: "*that it is largely governed by the nature of the client's locus of evaluation.* If that locus is markedly externalised the counsellor needs to be aware that the client will be vulnerable to any externally provided ways of defining himself." On the other hand, when the client has substantially internalized her "locus of evaluation" the counselor can trust the client to exert her own power in the relationship and take on a more active role.

Which path to travel?

When considering which path to take into the person-centered dreamsensing territory the answers to the following three questions are significant:

1. What are the needs of the client as she expresses them?
2. What does this particular dream bring?
3. What can the therapist offer?

What does the client need with regard to level of insight, level of safety, nature of therapist's input and support? What does this particular dream bring with regard to, for example, strength of emotional upheaval (anxiety, peacefulness, puzzlement …); is it a recurring nightmare, or part of a series of dreams; is a connection to a waking life issue evident or unclear? What the therapist can offer will on the one hand be dependent on the answers to the first two questions. On the other hand it will be dependent on what skills, experience and preference in methodology the therapist brings with her.

Let me dwell a bit more on the question of what the dream brings. Lemke presented her dreams in terms of a certain typology of dreams. Not intending to include all types of dreams and also stating that these categories sometimes overlap, she differentiates religious dreams, situational dreams, conflict dreams, recurring dreams, and series of dreams. Considering the complexity and potential multidimensionality with dreams I am skeptical about this typology. I would differentiate more along the line of what kind of initial "aura" the dream brings and the dreamer gives the dream. This will be very different if it is, for instance, a recurring dream bringing with it anxiety (like a nightmare) or if the recurring theme is something pleasant like flying. Considering that there is an ongoing process of interweaving and of mutual influencing between dreaming and waking life, probably all dreams are related to waking life issues. This of course will be even more evident when the dreamer is going through some sort of life-changing transition like a pregnancy, birth, death etc. (see Siegel, 2002). (For example, all of the dreams I presented in Chapter 3 are also connected to the current waking life project of writing this book. Also, the initial "aura" of the last dream was definitely more anxiety-prone than the first two.) In addition, it is most likely that on some level the dream touches on a conflict or ambivalence in the inner or outer world of the dreamer (as it did in all three of my dreams).

In this sense one could choose any of the levels of insight that Hill suggests in her model (and several more) with the same dream and most likely come up with relevant insights on all (i.e., the experiential, waking life, inner personality dynamics). All dreams arise in an ongoing process, so they are all part of a lifelong series of dreams. However, there are sometimes sequences of dreams where the dreamer easily sees either the connection in the story, or the theme between different dreams. Such relating can be of special interest because here one senses into the evolving process, into the changes happening from one dream to the next. This is particularly relevant when the series connects to the development of the therapy process or the accompanying life changes.

Summary of the chapter

Which path to choose is not a question that is easily answered or one that comes with just one answer. It depends on the client, the particular dream and on the therapist herself. In Chapter 2 I described how clients and therapists can differ with regard to their valuing of dreams and their experiencing of dreamsensing. I also pointed out the importance of the safety issue considering the fact that the therapist is guiding through a landscape that is often (for both client and therapist) foreign and vague. Safety can be enhanced by a high-quality relationship, by giving the session some extra structure or by moving forward at a slow Focusing pace. I believe any person-centered way of being with a client and her dream will lead to vital and creative insights. Apart from that I agree with Hill that it can also be lots of fun!

Concluding Thoughts

Having grown up spending part of my childhood in the USA (from ages 3 to 4 and 8 to 15), I have had early and extensive experience in making sense of a foreign culture and in effect bringing two worlds together. I know how it is to feel utterly alienated, not understanding anything of what is spoken. And on the other hand, also very well known to me is the feeling that when all has turned familiar, it then becomes difficult in retrospect to grasp that initial sense of not understanding.

This seems to have become a life pattern for me, venturing out and finding a foreign territory and slowly, painstakingly – but also with a lot of joy and curiosity – exploring and understanding it. Exploring my inner world – specifically my dreaming world – is one such venture. I sometimes look back and find it hard to believe that there was a time when I experienced my dreams in such an intense way that upon waking the first thing I did was blame my partner for all the things she had done to me in the dream. She pointed out the fact that it was my dream, a product of my imagination. It really took a while for this to sink in. Many years of dream journaling and dream study later, it still helps me to remember this once-experienced state when I teach others about to enter their dreaming world; it reminds me that we all start from different places.

When you enter into a foreign country it helps to have the support of a confident, experienced companion. Your curiosity and joy in the endeavor will be heightened if you have a feeling of safety. This kind of accompaniment is even more important, the more foreign this new country seems. If you are coming to this country in a hurt or anxious state, then the foreign language or the unfamiliarity with the way the people are acting will most likely provoke more anxiety than puzzlement. A confident companion by your side, who knows (or seems to know) where to go will give you a feeling of safety while traversing an unknown terrain. Next to the quality of relationship with the companion and the growing sense of trust in her capabilities, a certain structure to your journey can help your orientation. Also, a slowing of the pace may make you feel safer, letting you come to your senses every now and then and giving you a chance to let it all settle.

When you have traversed this foreign territory for some time and have merged two worlds within yourself, you may sometimes forget that people in the "outer world" aren't following the same path (for example, I sometimes actually forget that not everyone in Germany is as fluent in English as I am!). This can be an alienating experience, especially if one of the worlds you are carrying within is not represented or of interest in the "outer world." The dreaming world is generally not valued as such in most Western societies. There are of course significant differences within these societies, with certain "subcultures" being very aware and cherishing of the dreaming world (the "subculture" of therapy and counseling mirroring the broader culture in its diversity, with the person-centered approach hovering somewhere in the margins or "borderland," and Focusing having "one foot" inside of the dream territory).

Given the fact that I believe that the two processes of dreaming and Focusing have several significant similarities and can reinforce each other I have tried to bring more of the practice of Focusing "back" into person-centered theory and practice. Focusing can enhance dreamsensing (and with that, any form of therapy) tremendously; it can deepen and bring one closer to the original dream-experiencing itself. Gendlin's philosophy of change as most fully developed in his "Process Model" (1997a) could help to raise our philosophical understanding of what happens not only within therapy, but also during Focusing and during dreaming, both in and out of a formal therapeutic setting. Gendlin's main interest is to understand, explore and explain the process of Focusing. Thus, I am sorry to say, he has not integrated the dreaming process into his philosophy of the "Process Model." I have taken some baby steps in that direction elsewhere (see Koch, 2011) and hope to develop more profound ideas about this in the future.

Another intention of this book is to raise awareness of what has already been written about being with dreams in a person-centered way. Considering the fact that most of the literature has been in German, I wanted to feature at least one German-speaking person-centered authority on the subject. I understand that another book on a more structural person-centered way of being with dreams by Finke is presently a work in progress. I also am aware that since the writing of my master's thesis (Koch, 2007) quite a few students in Germany and Austria have taken up the subject of dreams. I hope that this book will help to generate future articles and books on person-centered ways of being with dreams.

I especially hope that more people, specifically in the academic field of person-centered research, will now want to look into Hill's impressive research record on working with dreams in therapy, and will be inspired to do similar research in the future. While reading about Hill's research design, results and consequent development of her model, I often was reminded of Rogers' pioneering steps into researching counseling and therapy. Hill has done equally pioneering research work with regard to working with dreams in therapy. I was also very impressed by Lemke's own research project, which she started when she was over seventy years old. Based on transcripts of many dream sessions and on finding her own sense of a person-centered way of being with dreams, Lemke's is an inspiring example for viable research outside of academia.

Sensing into dreams with groups in a person-centered way is another field that needs more attention and development. There are three promising models, one developed by Ullman (1996), one by Lawrence (2005) and one is a further development of the Hill model specifically for groups (see Wonnell, 2004). Both Ullman and Lawrence developed these models for groups primarily outside of a therapeutic setting, Ullman for self-help groups and Lawrence for the field of organizational development. I believe all three models can be easily adapted and integrated into a person-centered way of being with dreams and working with groups. On a slight sidetrack I want to mention Bosnak (2007), who has developed a therapeutic way of working with dreams in a group, termed "embodied dreamwork." Bosnak being a Jungian psychoanalyst, his approach is not easily adapted to a person-centered way of being, but it can provide stimulating ideas, especially for including Focusing in group dreamwork.

With this book I have sought to bring together the person-centered world with the dreaming world. I realize there is still some distance to go before this merging becomes so matter of fact that we can't imagine dreams ever not having been a part of person-centered theory and practice. Hence I want to close with a vision of how "it should be," how it would be if we had already arrived at this point. In what is, I hope, the near future, clients wanting to understand their dreams would know that they can go to person-centered therapists and would find as experienced and knowledgeable guides in this field as in other therapeutic orientations (e.g., psychodynamic or Gestalt). Sensing into dreams would be an integral part of training in person-centered counseling. Accordingly the literature grounding the further (theoretical and practical) development of the approach would feature dreamsensing as a significant part of exploring the inner world of the client – and of the therapist (as for instance Mearns, 2003 has done with Focusing). Furthermore, at the biennial international World Association for Person-Centered and Experiential Psychotherapy and Counseling (WAPCEPC) conferences there would be encounter groups sensing into their dreams starting off the mornings. The following sessions would include dreamsensing naturally as one perspective to be considered and there would be special sessions featuring the latest results of the many research projects on sensing into dreams.

Appendix A

Basics of the person-centered approach and Focusing

Person-centered approach

Carl Rogers (1902–1987) was the founder of the person-centered approach. He developed an approach to psychotherapy and counseling that, at the time (1940s–1960s), was considered quite radical. It is often situated within the humanistic tradition in psychotherapy, a third path distinct from psychoanalysis and behaviorism.

Rogers described his approach originally as nondirective and moved away from the more medical model, where the therapist is the expert healer, to a model where the client leads the way, trusting the inherent tendency (the actualizing tendency) of human beings to strive toward the fulfillment of their potentials. Rogers (1957) postulated six conditions that were necessary and sufficient for therapy to be successful: (1) both persons are in psychological contact; (2) the client is in a state of incongruence, being vulnerable or anxious; (3) the therapist is congruent; (4) the therapist experiences unconditional positive regard for the client; (5) the therapist experiences an empathic understanding of the client; (6) the client perceives, at least to a minimal degree, the conditions 4 and 5.

Originally developed as a concept for psychotherapy, Rogers and his colleagues went further and transferred the ideas to other areas where people are in relationships. For example in education, management, conflict resolution, and childcare (see also Appendix C for further reading references).

Focusing

Eugene Gendlin was an early close associate of Rogers, joining him in extensive groundbreaking research on psychotherapy. Looking at therapy transcripts and listening to tapes, Gendlin made a remarkable discovery: One could already identify, in their first session, the clients who went on to have a successful therapy. What set them apart was a special way of pausing, of sensing within. Gendlin found and elaborated a way to teach people this special way of inner bodily sensing, which he called Focusing. Gendlin also set about to understand and explain the Focusing process on a philosophical level and developed a philosophy of change. Bohart (2007, p. 267) describes the philosophical theory behind Focusing well:

> To understand Gendlin we need to go beyond the standard Western dichotomy between thoughts and feelings (feelings meaning emotions). For Gendlin, meanings are not only thoughts. There are also meanings that are experienced in the body, which he called "bodily felt" meanings.
>
> From Gendlin's (1996, 1997b) point of view we understand more at the experiential level than we do at the level of explicitly conceptualized knowledge. If one were to diagram these two, a broader circle would represent experiential knowing, and a smaller circle inside would represent knowledge that has been articulated into language. Gendlin's level of experiential knowing is in a class of related concepts, including tacit knowing. What is different about Gendlin's view is that although typical views of tacit knowing reserve sophistication for explicit conceptual knowing, and see tacit knowing as automatized, for Gendlin, experiential knowing is more finely textured and more complex than what has been incorporated into verbal knowledge structures. Effective insights are those that arise from a process of tuning into felt experience

and finding the right words to articulate it. The process of finding the right words leads to a felt shift. The new understanding is not just a discrete piece of knowledge. Rather, the process of attaining it already changes how the person experiences self and world. Gendlin called the process "focusing" and developed a procedure for fostering it.

Appendix B

Biographical notes on Lemke, McGavin, and Hill

Helga Lemke

Helga Lemke studied psychology, theology and pedagogy. Most of her professional life as a professor, she focused on teaching the person-centered approach to students of church and pastoral professions, as well as to medical doctors. Prior to the time her book *Das Traumgespräch* (Dream Conversation) was published in 2000, she had already written four other books on person-centered pastoral psychology and pastoral care. Some years after her retirement she became intrigued by dream conversations. Someone came to her with a recurring nightmare. The dreamer had been plagued with this dream since his childhood. Within one dream session Helga Lemke helped him to understand what the dream was trying to say. After this the dream never returned. This experience left such a lasting impression on her that she decided to study the possibilities of sensing into dreams during therapy and counseling sessions. For a year, she encouraged her clients to share their dreams. In the traditional "Rogerian way," she transcribed the sessions and tried to identify the aspects that helped the dreamer find an understanding of the dream and the things that blocked or hindered such a process. Subsequently she wrote up her research findings, writing the first book on working with dreams in a person-centered way. Staying true to her background in teaching pastoral carers and medical doctors, she stresses the fact that dream conversations can be helpful in many settings, not only therapy sessions but also within short medical consultations or pastoral settings.

Barbara McGavin

Barbara McGavin has been practicing Focusing since 1983 and is the co-founder of The British Focusing Network. She teaches Focusing full time and is a Certifying Coordinator for the international Focusing Institute in New York. Since 1994 she has developed – together with Ann Weiser Cornell – a special form of Focusing called "Inner Relationship Focusing." Also with Weiser Cornell, McGavin has co-authored *The Focusing Student's and Companion's Manual*, which is used by many Focusing teachers as a training manual. For quite a while McGavin gave workshops on dreams and Focusing, more recently concentrating on integrating Focusing within creative processes. She has a wide background in humanistic psychology, teaching, fine art and graphic design. McGavin strives to help people learn Focusing in the most enjoyable and effective way possible and encourages them to integrate Focusing into their daily lives.

Clara Hill

Clara E. Hill earned her Ph.D. in counseling psychology from Southern Illinois University in 1974. She started as an assistant professor in the Counseling Psychology Program in the Department of Psychology at the University of Maryland, where she is currently professor and co-director of the Maryland Psychotherapy Clinic and Research Lab. Next to working with dreams her areas of interest are the identification and training of counseling skills, process and outcome studies of psychotherapy, and qualitative research. She has written ten books, *Working with Dreams in Psychotherapy* being her third, and *Dream Work in Therapy: Facilitating Exploration, Insight, and Action* her sixth. In addition, she has written over 240 journal articles and book chapters and has been distinguished with many awards for her enormous contributions to psychology and psychotherapy research. She pioneered doing research on the effectiveness of dreamwork within therapy – and still to this day, she is one of the few researchers in this particular field.

Appendix C

Further resources

Books

I have read many invigorating books of which only a small collection made it into the reference section. The first two to inflame my dreaming passion were from Patricia Garfield (*Creative Dreaming*) and Ann Faraday (*The Dream Game*); both are still great introductions into the wonderful dream world. Carl Rogers' books are an enjoyable and easy read: I would suggest either starting with his last book *A Way of Being* or with a collection of his writings found in the *Carl Rogers Reader*. For more contemporary introductions to person-centered counseling I recommend the book by Mearns and Thorne (*Person-Centred Counselling in Action*), and by Mearns (*Developing Person-Centred Counselling*). Ann Weiser Cornell's books (*The Power of Focusing; The Radical Acceptance of Everything*) give a good introduction into general Focusing and "Inner Relationship Focusing." Campbell Purton's book (*Person-Centred Therapy: The Focusing-Oriented Approach*) gives a thorough introduction to both approaches and their integration.

Websites

- The website of *The International Association for the Study of Dreams* is a great entry point into the world of dream cherishers: http://www.asdreams.org/
- The website of *The World Association for Person-Centered and Experiential Psychotherapy and Counseling* is a good start in

navigating through the person-centered world: http://www.pce-world.org/

- The website of the *Focusing Institute* is very valuable for everything about Focusing, including an online library of all of Gendlin's written work: http://www.focusing.org/

References

Barrett-Lennard, G. T. (2003). *Steps on a mindful journey: Person-centred expressions.* Ross-on-Wye, UK: PCCS Books.

Barrett, D., & McNamara, P. (Eds.). (2007). *The new science of dreaming. Vol. 1: Biological aspects.* Westport, CT: Praeger.

Blechner, M. (2001). *The dream frontier.* Hillsdale, NJ: The Analytic Press.

Bohart, A. C. (2007). Insight and the active client. In L. G. Castonguay & C. E. Hill (Eds.), *Insight in psychotherapy* (pp. 257–277). Washington, DC: American Psychological Association.

Bohart, A. C. (2008). How clients self-heal in psychotherapy. In B. E. Levitt (Ed.), *Reflections on human potential: Bridging the person-centered approach and positive psychology* (pp. 175–186). Ross-on-Wye, UK: PCCS Books.

Bohart, A. C., & Tallman, K. (1999). *How clients make therapy work: The process of active self-healing.* Washington, DC: American Psychological Association.

Bosnak, R. (2007). *Embodiment: Creative imagination in medicine, art, and travel.* New York: Routledge.

Brown, B. (2007). *I thought it was just me (but it isn't).* New York: Gotham Books.

Bulkeley, K., & Bulkley, P. (2005). *Dreaming beyond death.* Boston: Beacon Press.

Conradi, P. (2000). Dreams, the unconscious and the person-centred approach: Revisioning practice. In T. Merry (Ed.), *Person-centred practice: The BAPCA reader* (pp. 218–231). Ross-on-Wye, UK: PCCS Books.

Coulson, A. (2000). The person-centred approach and the reinstatement of the unconscious. In T. Merry (Ed.), *Person-centred practice: The BAPCA reader* (pp. 208–217). Ross-on-Wye, UK: PCCS Books.

Dawson, T. (2000). Traum und TräumerIn. In H.-J. Feuerstein, D. Müller, & A. Weiser Cornell (Eds.), *Focusing im Prozess. Ein Lesebuch* (pp. 62–74). Köln: GwG-Verlag.

Ellingham, I. (2002). Madness and mysticism in perceiving the other: Towards a radical organismic, person-centred interpretation. In G. Wyatt & P. Sanders (Eds.), *Rogers' therapeutic conditions: Evolution, theory and practice. Vol. 4: Contact and perception* (pp. 234–258). Ross-on-Wye, UK: PCCS Books.

Faraday. A. (1974). *The dream game.* New York: Harper & Row.

Finke, J. (1990). Dream work in client-centered psychotherapy. In G. Lietaer, J. Rombauts & R. van Balen (Eds.), *Client-centered and experiential psychotherapy in the nineties* (pp. 503–510). Leuven, Belgium: Leuven University Press.

Finke, J. (1994). *Empathie und Interaktion.* Stuttgart: Thieme

Finke, J. (2004). *Gesprächspsychotherapie: Grundlagen und Spezifische Anwendungen.* Stuttgart: Thieme.

Fromm, E. (1951). *The forgotten language. An introduction to the understanding of dreams, fairy tales and myths.* New York: Rinehart & Co.

Garfield, P. (1995) *Creative dreaming* (2nd ed.). New York: Fireside.

Gendlin, E. T. (1986). *Let your body interpret your dreams.* Wilmette, IL: Chiron Publications.

Gendlin, E. T. (1992). Three learnings since the dreambook. *The Folio: A Journal for Focusing and Experiential Therapy, (11)*1, 25–30.

Gendlin, E. T. (1996). *Focusing-oriented psychotherapy: A manual of the experiential method.* New York: Guilford Press.

Gendlin, E. T. (1997a). *A process model.* New York: The Focusing Institute.

Gendlin, E. T. (1997b). *Experiencing and the creation of meaning: A philosophical and psychological approach to the subjective.* Evanston, IL: Northwestern University Press.

Gendlin, E. T. (2012, in press). Body dreamwork. In D. Barrett & P. McNamara (Eds.), *Encyclopedia of Sleep and Dreams.* Santa Barbara, CA: Greenwood.

Gerl, W. (1981). Mit Träumen arbeiten – dort wo der Klient ist. *GwG–Info, 45*, 35–38.

Graessner, D. (1989). Traumbearbeitung und Focusing. *GwG Zeitschrift, 74*, 43–48.

Hartmann, E. (2001). *Dreams and nightmares. The origin and meaning of dreams* (4th ed.). Cambridge, MA: Perseus Publishers.

Heaton, K. J. (2004). Working with nightmares. In C. E. Hill (Ed.), *Dream work in therapy. Facilitating exploration, insight, and action* (pp. 203–222). Washington, DC: American Psychological Association.

Hess, S. A. (2004). Dreams of the bereaved. In C. E. Hill (Ed.), *Dream work in therapy. Facilitating exploration, insight, and action* (pp. 169–185). Washington, DC: American Psychological Association.

Hill, C. E. (1996). *Working with dreams in psychotherapy.* New York: Guilford Press.

Hill, C. E. (Ed.). (2004). *Dream work in therapy. Facilitating exploration, insight, and action.* Washington, DC: American Psychological Association.

Hill, C. E. (2009). *Helping skills: Facilitating exploration, insight and action* (3rd ed.). Washington, DC: American Psychological Association.

Hill, C. E., & Knox, S. (2010). The use of dreams in modern psychotherapy. *International Review of Neurobiology, 92*, 291–317.

Hill, C. E., & Spangler, P. (2007). Dreams and psychotherapy. In D. Barrett & P. McNamara (Eds.), *The new science of dreaming. Vol. 2: Content, recall, and personality correlates* (pp. 159–186). Westport, CT: Praeger.

Iberg, J. R. (1996). Finding the body's next step: Ingredients and hindrances. *The Folio: A Journal for Focusing and Experiential Therapy, 15*(1), 13–42.

Jennings, J. L. (1986). The dream is the dream is the dream. A person-centered approach to dream analysis. *Person-Centered Review, 1*(3), 310–333.

Jennings, J. L. (1995). Dream-centered dream study: The pursuit of prolucidity. *Journal of Mental Imagery, 19*(1&2), 43–66.

Jung, C. G. (1990). Allgemeine Gesichtspunkte zur Psychologie des Traumes. In *Traum und Traumdeutung* (pp. 89–131). München: Deutscher Taschenbuch Verlag. (Original work published 1916)

Keil, W. W. (2002). Der Traum in der Klientenzentrierten Psychotherapie. In W. W. Keil & G. Stumm (Eds.), *Die vielen Gesichter der Personzentrierten Psychotherapie* (pp. 427–443). Wien: Springer Verlag.

Klingenbeck, P. (1998). Klientenzentrierte Traumarbeit. *Brennpunkt Sondernummer zur Fachtagung 1996*, 84–87.

Koch, A. (2007). *Traumerleben und Traumgespräch in der Personzentrierten Beratung.* Unpublished master's thesis. FernUniversität, Hagen, Germany.

Koch, A. (2009a). Dreams: Bringing us two steps closer to the client's perspective. *Person-Centered & Experiential Psychotherapies, 8*(4), 333–348.

Koch, A. (2009b). Workshop: Traumerleben und Traumgespräche. *Gesprächspsychotherapie und Personzentrierte Beratung, 40*(3), 138–140.

Koch, A. (2011). The interweaving of dreaming and focusing. *The Focusing Connection, 28*(6), 3.

Korbei, L. (2002). Zur Einbeziehung des Körpers in die Klientenzentrierte/ Personzentrierte Psychotherapie: Zwei Perspektiven. Perspektive 1: Der einbezogene Körper. In W. W. Keil & G. Stumm (Eds.), *Die vielen Gesichter der Personzentrierten Psychotherapie* (pp. 377–389). Wien: Springer Verlag.

Krippner, S., Bogzaran, F., & Carvalho, A. P. D. (2002). *Extraordinary dreams and how to work with them.* Albany, NY: State University of New York Press.

Lawrence, W. G. (2005). *Introduction to social dreaming. Transforming thinking.* London: Karnac.

Leijssen, M. (2004). Focusing-oriented dream work. In R. I. Rosner, W. J. Lyddon, & A. Freeman (Eds.), *Cognitive therapy and dreams* (pp. 137–160). New York: Springer.

Lemke, H. (2000). *Das Traumgespräch. Umgang mit Träumen nach klientenzentriertem Konzept.* Stuttgart: Kohlhammer.

Mearns, D. (1997). *Person-centred counselling training.* London: Sage.

Mearns, D. (2003). *Developing person-centred counselling* (2nd ed.). London: Sage.

Mearns, D., & Cooper, M. (2005). *Working at relational depth in counselling and psychotherapy* (2nd ed.). London: Sage.

Mearns, D., & Thorne, B. (2007). *Person-centred counselling in action* (3rd ed.). London: Sage.

Pascual-Leone, A., & Greenberg, L. S. (2007). Insight and awareness in experiential therapy. In L. G. Castonguay & C. E. Hill (Eds.), *Insight in psychotherapy* (pp. 31–56). Washington, DC: American Psychological Association.

Pfeiffer, W. M. (1989). Arbeit mit Träumen – ein zentrales Thema des Kongresses in Leuven 1988. *GwG Zeitschrift, 74,* 68–70.

Purton, C. (2004). *Person-centred therapy. The focusing-oriented approach.* Houndmills, UK: Palgrave Macmillan.

Rogers, C. R. (1951). *Client-centered therapy: Its current practice, implications, and theory.* Boston: Houghton Mifflin.

Rogers, C. R. (1957). The necessary and sufficient conditions of therapeutic personality change. *Journal of Consulting Psychology, 21* (2), 95–103. Reprinted in H. Kirschenbaum & V. L. Henderson (Eds.). (1989). *The Carl Rogers reader* (pp. 219–235). Boston: Houghton Mifflin.

Rogers, C. R. (1961). *On becoming a person* (2nd ed.). Boston: Houghton Mifflin.

Rogers, C. R. (1977). *Carl Rogers on personal power.* New York: Delacorte Press.

Rogers, C. R. (1980). *A way of being.* Boston: Houghton Mifflin.

Rogers, C. R., & Sanford, R. (1989). Client-centered psychotherapy. In H. I. Kaplan & B. J. Sadock (Eds.), *Comprehensive textbook of psychiatry, Vol. 2* (pp. 1482–1501). Baltimore, MD: Williams & Wilkins.

Sanders, P., & Wyatt, G. (2002). The history of conditions one and six. In G. Wyatt & P. Sanders (Eds.), *Rogers' therapeutic conditions: Evolution, theory and practice. Vol. 4: Contact and perception* (pp. 1–24). Ross-on-Wye, UK: PCCS Books.

Schmid, P. F. (1992). "Die Traumkunst träumt, und alle Zeichen trügen." Der Traum als Encounter und Kunstwerk. In P. Frenzel, P. F. Schmid, & M. Winkler (Eds.), *Handbuch der Personzentrierten Psychotherapie* (pp. 391–409). Köln: Edition Humanistische Psychologie.

Schredl, M., Bohusch, C., Kahl, J., Mader, A., & Somesan, A. (2000). The use of dreams in psychotherapy: A survey of psychotherapists in private practice. *The Journal of Psychotherapy Practice and Research, 9*, 81–87.

Siegel, A. (2002). *Dream wisdom. Uncovering life's answers in your dreams.* Berkeley, CA: Celestial Arts.

Stolte, S., & Koch, S. (1992). *Der Umgang mit Träumen in der klientenzentrierten Psychotherapie.* Unpublished master's thesis. Technische Universität Braunschweig, Germany.

Stumm, G. (1992). Ich kann mich jetzt besser leiden. Interpretationsebenen des therapeutischen Prozesses. In P. Frenzel, P. F. Schmid, & M. Winkler (Eds.), *Handbuch der Personzentrierten Psychotherapie* (pp. 241–262). Köln: Edition Humanistische Psychologie.

Taylor, J. (1992). *Where people fly and water runs uphill: Using dreams to tap the wisdom of the unconscious.* New York: Warner Books.

Teichmann-Wirth, B. (2002). Zur Einbeziehung des Körpers in die Klientenzentrierte/Personzentrierte Psychotherapie: Zwei Perspektiven. Perspektive 2: Der einzubeziehende Körper. In W. W. Keil & G. Stumm (Eds.), *Die vielen Gesichter der Personzentrierten Psychotherapie* (pp. 387–410). Wien: Springer Verlag.

Thorne, B. (2003). *Carl Rogers* (2nd ed.). London: Sage.

Tudor, K., & Worrall, M. (2006). *Person-centred therapy. A clinical philosophy.* Hove, UK: Routledge.

Ullman, M. (1996). *Appreciating dreams: A group approach.* Thousand Oaks, CA: Sage.

Vossen, T. (1988). Taumtherapie – personenzentriert. *GwG-Zeitschrift, 74,* 30–43.

Vossen, T. (1990). Client-centered dream therapy. In G. Lietaer, J. Rombauts, & R. Van Balen (Eds.), *Client-centered and experiential psychotherapy in the nineties* (pp. 511–548). Leuven, Belgium: Leuven University Press.

Wamsley, E., & Antrobus, J. S. (2007). Dream production: A neural network attractor, dual rhythm regional cortical activation, homeostatic model. In D. Barrett & P. McNamara (Eds.), *The new science of dreaming. Vol. 1: Biological aspects* (pp. 156–183). Westport, CT: Praeger.

Weiser Cornell, A. (1996). *The power of focusing: A practical guide to emotional self-healing.* Oakland, CA: New Harbinger.

Weiser Cornell, A. (2005). *The radical acceptance of everything. Living a focusing life.* Berkeley, CA: Caluna Press.

Wijngaarden, H. R. (1991). Traum, geführter Tagtraum und active Imagination in der klientenzentrierten Psychotherapie. In J. Finke & L. Teusch (Eds.), *Gesprächspsychotherapie bei Neurosen und psychosomatischen Erkrankungen* (pp. 187–195). Heidelberg, Germany: Asanger.

Wonnell, T. L. (2004). Working with dreams in groups. In C. E. Hill (Ed.), *Dream work in therapy. Facilitating exploration, insight, and action* (pp. 115–132). Washington, DC: American Psychological Association.

Index